contents

Contents

Foreword

Beverley Bernard

If democracy depends on informed public opinion, we need to ask what service the media provides. We need to consider and understand that the media is setting the agenda and not simply reflecting what happens in our society. The media itself chooses to understate its own power and influence in leading change.

The media has a responsibility to help ensure that Britain is a diverse society which works for all its members. This guide stems from a recognition that this responsibility goes wider than just what media organisations say in their pages of newsprint or on the air. They have a corporate role to play as well.

One would hope that all major media players will recognise good practice and approach their responsibilities in the way that ITV has in producing this excellent guide.

Whatever your reason for reading this guide, don't leave it to gather dust on the shelf. It should be used to actively promote and celebrate diversity at every opportunity.

Beverley Bernard
Deputy Chair, Commission for Racial Equality

Introduction

Charles Allen CBE

Michael Green

Welcome to this ITV guide on Cultural Diversity. As the largest commercial broadcaster in the UK we broadcast across the 14 distinct regions of the UK from our 15 regional television licences – Anglia, Border, Carlton London, Carlton Central, Carlton West Country, Channel, Grampian, Granada, HTV, LWT, Meridian, Scottish, Tyne Tees, Ulster and Yorkshire Television.

ITV is a founder member of the Cultural Diversity Network, set up to change the face of television, ensuring it responds to Britain's increasingly multi-racial society. We are personally committed to ensuring that all our ITV licences build, develop and reflect relationships with the diverse communities across our regions in our programming and initiatives both on and off screen.

We piloted this concise guide in our Meridian licence, the ITV company serving the South and South East of England, where it proved very successful.

It does not claim to answer all the questions, nor does it seek to explain all the differences. What it does aim to do is unravel some mysteries and to explode some myths to enable the reader to have a clearer understanding of how the beliefs of others impact on the way they live their lives. It aims to help people from diverse faiths and cultures to live and work together without causing offence through ignorance and to nurture tolerance and respect through understanding. It has been researched and written by members of the various faith communities and as such represents their views. This guide is only a starting point. We hope you find it informative.

Charles Allen CBE
Executive Chairman
Granada plc

Michael Green
Chairman
Carlton Communications plc

african caribbean

African Caribbean

The African Caribbean (Black) community embraces many faiths including Islam, Buddhism, Rastafarianism and Christianity. The latter includes many denominations such as the Methodists, Seventh Day Adventists, Spiritual Baptists, Baptists, the Church of England, and a range of Pentecostal denominations.

The most notable is Rastafarianism, not because of the level of participation, but because it is a faith specific to the African Caribbean (Black) community.

A Rastafarian is a person who believes in the divinity of the descendant of King Solomon, His Imperial Majesty Haile Selassie I of Ethiopia as the reincarnation of Christ as well as the embodiment of the Godhead.

Ras means *head*, Tafari means *God*. Ras Tafari (Amharic) means *Head Creator*.

An introduction to the faith

To outsiders, the Rastafari faith is still a cultural enigma at the dawn of the new millennium.

"In the space of 70 years since it's inception, Rastafari has outgrown its cult status in Jamaica to become one of the most influential contemporary religious movements."
(The Centenary Committee for Rastafari)

World membership of the Rastafari faith is now several million. In the last three decades Rastafari graduated from the traumas of persecution and attempted genocide in Jamaica during 1930 – 1960 to attracting a world audience

9

in the 70's, mainly through the music of mega-stars like Bob Marley who took the Rastafari message to a global audience.

'Marley's theology continues to live in the appropriations of Black Diaspora Music; it is highly significant that, for many weeks in the charts, the number one song was 'Killing Me Softly' by The Fugees who claim Bob Marley as their primary musical influence... they rework his social, and political critique and religious orientation' [Beckford 1998:129][1]

In health, diet, music, fashion, sport and youth culture, Rastafari ideology, outlook and colours have been 'adopted' by a world generation seeking a new and positive moral order. The dreadlocked image and lifestyle, once rejected and vilified by polite society has now become not just acceptable but a much emulated and admired style in the UK and beyond.

On the premise of the divinity of H.I.M. Haile Selassie, the Bible is the source of the Rastafarian way of life and faith. The Old Testament book of Leviticus defines living codes such as diet, conduct and lifestyle.

Hair in both men and women and beards are left uncut, the uncut locks being a sign of strength representing breaking away from the 'Babylonian' system of Western society. The uncut locks also represent the mane of the lion, the symbol of African strength and emancipation, and are kept covered by certain Rastas.

Nyabinghi reasoning sessions are a focal meeting point of Rasta communities involving drumming, reasoning

[1] Beckford, Robert (1998)
Jesus is Dread
Darton Longman & Todd, London

(discussions) and the smoking of the holy sacrament – ganga – a spiritual herb used for worship.

Many Rastas identify with the main guiding principles: "Peace & Love", "Truth & Rights".

Festivals

Many Rastas celebrate the Sabbath according to the Bible.

7th January is the Ethiopian Christmas popularly known as Rasmus.

The earthday (birthday) of His Imperial Majesty Emperor Haile Selassie on 23rd July 1892 is generally celebrated, as is his coronation as Emperor on 2nd November 1930.

Black liberation civil rights activist Marcus Garvey is considered an important figure for Rastafarians and his birthday on 17th August is widely celebrated.

Other significant religious events

Shashamane in Ethiopia is the sacred land granted by His Imperial Majesty Emperor Haile Selassie to the people of the African Diaspora to acknowledge support of the Motherland (Africa). Black people from the Western hemisphere could repatriate to build a secure Utopia for future generations.

Organisations who have helped to stamp the emergence of Rastafari in the new Millennium include the Ethiopian World Federation (EWF), a Rastafarian organisation that works to raise funds for pilgrimages to Shashamane. The London based Centenary Committee for Rastafari (CCR) organised the first international assembly in Ethiopia in 1992. This historic event celebrated the 100th anniversary of the birth of Emperor Haile Selassie I and the task of building a Tabernacle with the support of the inter-national community which today stands as a beacon on a hill calling the Rastafari faithful home to Mount Zion.

Birth customs

Babies born to Rastafarians are offered up to Jah (God) at birth. The child will be encouraged to follow the 'livity' (way of life) of Rasta.

Death customs and funeral rites

'Dead' and 'Death' are words considered negative and are rarely used by Rastafarians who follow the more widely believed positive concept of 'ever-living'. 'Passed' or 'passing' is used instead reinforcing the Rasta belief that life is eternal through the spirit. Rastafarians spend this life preparing for continuation into the next stating "I'n'I live on itinually" meaning life is eternal.

Diet

The term used as a model for idealised lifestyles of Rastafarians is 'Ital' meaning a saltless, vegetarian diet. 'Ital' also means natural food. Rastafarians shun eating the 'flesh of scavengers' like pork or shellfish, yet fish & fowl (chicken) are acceptable with many. Alcohol is discouraged. Those attending Nyabinghi ceremonies are expected to observe a strict ital diet for the duration, which can last up to a week.

Dress

Festivals and celebrations usually require women to cover their heads and to wear long dresses in earthy Rasta colours. Trousers are not acceptable and makeup is not encouraged.

The uncombed, uncut locks are the symbol of the devout Rasta and are seen as a sacrament, which many always have covered with a 'tam' (a large hat) or 'wrap' (a cloth wrapped into a turban).

African attire is encouraged especially in the red, gold and green colours of the Ethiopian flag. Mudcloth and Kente designs from Africa are popular.

Visitors may be asked to remove their shoes when entering a Rastafarian household.

Giving of gifts

Greetings	Traditionally Rastafarians greet each other with respect even if strangers. Globally Rastas will 'hail' each other by saying "Greetings", "Hail Ras" as a mark of respect.
Gifts	Afro-centric gifts are appreciated by Rastafarians. Crafted wood, Rasta imagery and colours which symbolise Rastafarian roots; red for the colour of the blood of man, gold for the sun and the wealth and green for nature and the land of Africa, are welcomed, as are the traditional fruit and flowers.

Main languages spoken

Amharic, the ancient language of Ethiopia, plays an important part in Rastafarian Liturgy

Patois – the language of the African Diaspora.

The reasoning language of Rastafari is the I'n'I, which eliminates all negative sounds replacing them with positive. The term 'I' represents God and therefore your people, your family and your beliefs.

Medical treatment

Some orthodox Rastafarians may refuse medical treatment of blood transfusions although more liberal Rastas may take all forms of treatment.

Rastas tend to be herbalists using natural methods of self-healing.

Homeopathy and African traditional cures are widely used.

Naming & naming ceremonies

A child is usually given an African or Biblical name at birth. This takes place at a naming ceremony when the child is a few months old. According to your Rasta tribe a child may be given a name according to the month of birth. This can be adopted later for the converted. The list starts with April, as this is the month Reuben – the first son of Jacob, father of Israel – was born.

Naming Table

Colour	Tribe	Month
Silver	Reuben	April
Gold	Simeon	May
Purple	Levi	June
Brown	Judah	July
Yellow	Issacher	August
Pink	Zebulon	September
Blue	Dan	October
Red	Gad	November
Grey	Asher	December
Green	Naphtali	January
White	Joseph	February
Black	Benjamin	March

Other

Rastafarians are divided into several different groups including The Nyabinghi Order, Twelve Tribes of Israel, Ethiopian World Federation, Bobo Dreads, Orthodox and more.

Ethiopian World Federation (EWF)	These Rastafarians only recognise the divinity of His Imperial Majesty, Emperor Haile Selassie I and will only accept those of African descent as true Rastas.
Twelve Tribes of Israel	Recognise the divinity of H.I.M. but also acknowledge his son as a descendent of King Solomon. All races are welcome as Rastas.
Bobo/Bubba Dread	Very strict orthodox Rastas whose philosophy stems from the preachings of the prophet Emmanuel. Heads are *always* covered with a white turban and codes of Rasta are stringently observed.
Ethiopian Orthodox Church	The state church of Ethiopia and the oldest Christian religion in the world has most Rastafarian members.

Glossary

Amharic	The language of the royal Ethiopian dynasty since the 13th century.
Babylon	From a Rastafari perspective, Babylon is the historically white – European colonial and imperialist power structure, which has oppressed Blacks and other peoples of colour.

Diaspora	The African Diaspora began in the early 16th century and displaced tens of millions of Africans from their ancestral continent (dispersion; a migration, the dispersion of an originally homogeneous people)
Elder	The term given to individuals of long-standing commitment in the Rasta Movement.
I'n'I	Me & mine, we.
Ital	Vital – meaning 'pure', 'natural', 'organic', Ital is a term for a saltless and vegetarian diet.
I-ses	Praises.
Iration	Creation.
Jah	In Rasta speech, this term is used as a synonym for Emperor Haile Selassie as the manifestation of the Godhead. The term derives from the Old Testament where it appears as an archaic form of "Jehovah" (see Psalm 68:4).
Nyabinghi	Derived from an African secret society, which operated in the Congo and Rwanda during the last quarter of 19th century, Nyabinghi refers to religious gatherings of Rasta brethren (men) and sistren (women) where dancing and drumming are commonplace.

Ras Tafari	The pre-coronation name of Emperor Haile Selassie I. Ras is an Amharic term meaning equivalent to Duke or Lord. Tafari Makonnen was the family name of Emperor Selassie.
Reasoning	An important recognition of the oral tradition of Rastafarian culture. Reasoning offers an opportunity for the exchange of ideas and information, religious teachings, history and story telling.
Reggae	Reflecting the basic rhythmic influences of Nyabinghi drumming as well as that of other African Jamaican musical traditions, reggae is the Rasta-inspired music of black protest originating in Jamaica in the 1960's and spreading the message of Rasta internationally to this day.
Spiritual Baptists	A religion based on a fusion of Christianity and African ritual beliefs developed by African slaves in the Caribbean.
Zion	Zion refers broadly to Africa and more specifically to Ethiopia as the ancestral homeland of all black peoples.

References

Beckford, R. (1998) *'Jesus is Dread'* London: Darton Longman & Todd

Owens, J. (1982) *'Dread Rastafarians of Jamaica'* Heinemann

The Centenary Committee for Rastafari
PO Box 8337, London W12 9WE

BOOM Publishing, Culture Mix Arts
PO Box 2766, Reading, Berkshire RG30 1RF
www.culturemixarts.co.uk

Special thanks to:

Mr & Mrs Carlos Holder
Mr A Guy
Mr S Taylor
Aqua Livi
Don John
Godfrey Brandt

Compiled by Mary Genis

bahá'í

Bahá'í

A Bahá'í is a member of the Bahá'í Faith who believe in the Prophet founder Bahá'u'lláh.

An introduction to the faith

The Bahá'í Faith is an independent world religion with approximately six million members world wide coming from virtually every nationality, religious background, ethnic group and social class.

The Prophet Founder of the Bahá'í Faith was Bahá'u'lláh, a Persian nobleman who suffered 40 years of imprisonment and exile. Bahá'ís believe that he was the latest in a line of Messengers from God that includes Abraham, Krishna, Moses, Buddha, Zoroaster, Christ and Muhammad.

The main theme of Bahá'u'lláh's message is unity. He taught that there is only one God, that all the world's religions represent one changeless and eternal Faith of God, and that all humanity is one race, destined to live in peace and harmony.

Bahá'ís work towards the creation of an ever-advancing, sustainable world civilisation, based on the principles of the oneness of humankind, equality of women and men; the elimination of all forms of prejudice, economic justice; universal education and the harmony of science and religion.

With significant communities in at least 233 countries and dependent territories, the Bahá'í Faith has become, in only a century, the second most widespread religion after Christianity and is among the fastest growing religions in the world.

Bahá'í Writings	Bahá'u'lláh himself wrote voluminously and Bahá'ís should read every morning and evening from His writings. Bahá'u'lláh's son and successor, 'Abdu'l-Bahá, was also the interpreter of Bahá'u'lláh's writings and wrote many volumes of books and tablets. Further Bahá'í writings came from 'Abdu'l-Bahá's grandson and Guardian of the Bahá'í Faith, Shoghi Effendi, who was the head of the Bahá'í world community after the passing of his grandfather in 1921 until his own death in London in 1957.
The Covenant	Bahá'u'lláh appointed 'Abdu'l-Bahá as his successor, making him the Centre of his Covenant and the head of the Bahá'í Community. By this appointment Bahá'u'lláh safeguarded and protected the religion against differences and schisms, making it impossible for anyone to create a new sect or faction or belief. This Covenant of Bahá'u'lláh is unique in religious history.

Festivals/holy days

The Bahá'í calendar is made up of 19 months consisting of 19 days in each month with the remaining days called the Intercalary Days, and celebrated as Ayyám-i-yá, a time for spiritual preparation for the fast, hospitality, feasting, charity and giving gifts.

The feast or festival of Ridván is a twelve-day festival commemorating Bahá'u'lláh's declaration of His mission to His companions and celebrated annually from 21st April until 2nd May. Bahá'u'lláh acclaimed Ridván as the 'Most Great Festival' and has referred to it as the Day whereon 'the breezes of forgiveness were wafted over the entire creation'.

The first, ninth and twelfth days of Ridván are celebrated as Holy Days on which work is suspended. Local Assemblies are elected on the first day of Ridván while national assemblies are elected during the Ridván period.

Naw-Rúz – literally, New Day – is the Bahá'í New Year which is celebrated on 21st March. In the Bahá'í calendar, Naw-Rúz falls on the day of Bahá of the month of Bahá. The festival of Naw-Rúz marks the end of the month of fasting and is a joyous time of celebration. It is a Bahá'í Holy Day on which work is suspended.

The anniversary of the birth of Bahá'u'lláh is on 12th November. Born Mírzá Husayn-'Alí in 1817 in Mázindarán, Persia (Iran) Bahá'í communities come together for celebration and fellowship.

There are no prescribed ceremonies for the commemoration of Holy Days, but many Bahá'í communities combine a devotional programme with fellowship or appropriate social activities.

Other significant religious events

Declaration of the Báb	23rd May
Ascension of Bahá'u'lláh	29th May
Martyrdom of the Báb	9th July
Birth of the Báb	20th October
Day of the Covenant	26th November
Ascension of 'Abdu'l-Bahá	28th November

Fasting (2 – 20 March) requires the abstinence from food and drink between sunrise and sunset. This is a period of meditation, prayer, spiritual recuperation and a symbolic reminder of abstinence from selfish and carnal desires. Fasting is only undertaken by those of the age of maturity (15 years).

Pilgrimage to the Bahá'í Holy Places in Haifa, Israel is obligatory for Bahá'ís if one can afford it and is able to do so.

Nineteen Day Feast. This marks the first day of the Bahá'í month, bringing together the Bahá'í community of the locality for worship, consultation and fellowship.

Birth customs

Bahá'ís have very few, if any, rituals. However, there is no objection to the giving of gifts on happy occasions in accordance with the traditions of the relevant culture of the country, as long as they adhere to certain dietary restrictions (see Diet).

Death customs and funeral rites

Bahá'ís believe that the body is the temple of the spirit and must be respected and treated with honour. In Bahá'í law cremation is forbidden and the body must not be transported more than one hour's journey from the place of death. The body is wrapped in a shroud of silk or cotton and a ring, bearing a specific inscription is placed on the deceased's finger. The body is placed in a coffin made of crystal, stone or hard, fine wood. A specific Prayer for the Dead is said before internment. Bahá'ís are instructed to write a will and are free to dispose of their wealth in any way they wish.

Diet

There are no dietary requirements for Bahá'ís to follow but Bahá'ís would have to decline any invitations of food or drink during the fasting period (March 2 – 20 between sunrise and sunset). It is not appropriate to give or offer Bahá'ís a gift of, or any foods containing, alcohol as it is a Bahá'í law to abstain from alcohol and from the use of non-medicinal drugs as they believe both practices are harmful to physical and spiritual health.

Dress

Bahá'ís do not have any form of dress requirements other than to practice moderation and modesty.

Giving of gifts

There are no particular customs or rituals in the Bahá'í faith regarding giving gifts or greetings (other than those mentioned above), just appropriate social behaviour for the relevant event or for the customs of the culture of the country of residence.

Main languages spoken

The main language for Bahá'ís is the spoken language of the country of residence.

Medical treatment

The Bahá'í teachings see human beings as both physical and spiritual in nature and believe that health is achieved when there is well-being and balance in both those aspects of a person's life. When ill, Bahá'ís seek medical treatment from a qualified physician. The use of contraception is restricted to methods that do not terminate the pregnancy after conception as Bahá'ís believe that the soul comes into being at conception.

Names and naming ceremonies

The Bahá'í teachings do not provide for any formal naming and there is no baptismal service. However there is no objection to Bahá'ís coming together to celebrate such happy occasions, provided they do not hold an official public ceremony.

There are no religious titles. Bahá'ís follow the customs of their country of residence as to the taking of a name at marriage and in the form of address appropriate for introduction, for example in the UK: Mr., Mrs., Miss., Ms., Dr., etc.

Other

In a Bahá'í marriage each partner must freely choose the other and once the choice is made, the consent of the living, natural parents of both parties is needed to help create unity between the two families.

Bahá'ís do not have pictures of Bahá'u'lláh. It would be inappropriate to try to represent Bahá'u'lláh in any form, artistic or otherwise.

Bahá'ís are required to obey the government and abstain from partisan politics as it is believed partisan politics create disunity in the community. Backbiting and gossiping are forbidden because they cause division.

At present, Bahá'ís in most localities have no special place of worship, they meet either in each other's homes or at a Bahá'i centre. It is envisaged, however, that in the future there will be a House of Worship (Bahá'i temple) in each town.

The Bahá'í House of Worship is open to people of different races, religious backgrounds and nationalities, not just Bahá'ís, in accordance with the Bahá'í aim of fostering unity. At present there are seven Houses of Worship around the world, close to Chicago USA; Kampala, Uganda; Sydney, Australia; Frankfurt, Germany; Panama City, Panama; Apia, Samoa; and in New Delhi, India.

Bahá'í Words

Please take note of the spelling of Bahá'í words. Often the words are Persian in origin and thus have unusual accents, for example in the word Bahá'í. Where possible do use the correct spelling.

Glossary

Bahá'í Word	Translation	Explanation
'Abdu'l-Bahá	Servant of Bahá	Eldest surviving Son of Bahá'u'lláh and His designated successor (1844 – 1921).
The Báb	The Gate	Forerunner of Bahá'u'lláh and Prophet Founder of the Bábi Faith (1819 – 1850).
Bahá'í		A follower of Bahá'u'llah.
Bahá'í World Centre		Spiritual and Administrative centre of the Bahá'í Faith in Haifa, Israel, comprising the Holy Places in Haifa and Akká and the administrative buildings on Mount Carmel.
Bahá'í International Community		The official name of the world wide Bahá'í community in its relations to outside organisations with offices at the United Nations in New York City, USA and in Geneva, Switzerland.
Bahá'u'lláh	Glory of God	Prophet Founder of Bahá'í Faith and the Manifestation of God for this Day (1817 – 1892).
Fireside		A meeting held in one's home for the purpose of teaching the Bahá'í Faith.

Bahá'í Word	Translation	Explanation
Funds		Money is voluntarily contributed by the Bahá'ís to the different institutions of the Faith. Contributions are not accepted from non-Bahá'ís.
Guardian, The		Shoghi Effendi, Grandson of 'Abdu'l-Bahá and head of the Bahá'í World from 1921 to his passing in 1957.
Kitábi-i-Aqdas	Most Holy Book	Bahá'u'lláh's book of laws, revealed in Akká in 1873. It sets forth ordinances of Bahá'u'lláh's Dispensation, but is much more than a mere code of laws.
Local Spiritual Assembly		The local administrative body of the Bahá'í Faith elected annually from among the body of believers in a community.
Manifestation/ Messenger of God		The Great Prophets of God, God's chosen messengers, who appear in each age.
National Spiritual Assembly		The National Administrative body of the Bahá'í Faith. Elected annually by delegate representatives of the local communities. Responsible for the affairs of the national Bahá'í community.

Bahá'í Word	Translation	Explanation
Obligatory Prayer		The daily recital of one of three specific prayers revealed by Bahá'u'lláh is binding on Bahá'ís from the age of maturity, which is fifteen years.
Universal House of Justice		Supreme administrative body of the Bahá'í Faith, elected every five years by member of the National Spiritual Assemblies.

Further information

National Spiritual Assembly of the Bahá'ís of the United Kingdom

27 Rutland Gate
London SW7 1PD
Tel: 020 7584 2566
Fax: 020 7584 9402
Email: oea@bahai.org.uk
Website: www.bahai.org.uk

For local Bahá'í Communities visit the above website, look in Yellow Pages or call the Bahá'í Information Office on 01732 373759.

Further reading

Bahá'í Publishing Trust

6 Mount Pleasant
Oakham
Leicestershire LE15 6HU
Tel: 01572 722780
Fax: 01572 724 280
Email: sales@bahaibooks.co.uk

Compiled by the Bahá'í Community of the United Kingdom.

buddhism

Buddhism

A Buddhist is a person who accepts a) the Buddha, b) the Buddha's teaching and c) the Buddha's followers who have achieved enlightenment. These are known as the "Three Jewels", or three main guides through life. Buddhism, like most of the great religions of the world, is divided into a number of different traditions and there are two main schools of Buddhism: The Theravada, or "Teaching of The Elders", and Mahayana, or "Greater Vehicle".

33

An introduction to the faith

The Buddha was an Indian prince who around 2500 years ago, after many years of searching for a way to free himself and those he loved from the suffering of old age, sickness and death; discovered enlightenment. For the next forty-five years he instructed those who were willing to listen in the method to achieve enlightenment for themselves.

He taught what he called The Four Noble Truths: first, that all life is unsatisfactory, second that this springs from our craving. Complete happiness can be gained by the third, which is the absolute elimination of craving. This is achieved by the fourth Noble Truth, which comprises following what Buddhists refer to as The Noble Eightfold Path i.e. the path of right understanding, right thought, right speech, right action, right livelihood, right effort, right mindfulness and right concentration. All eight components of this path are required to be developed together in order to achieve full enlightenment.

From India, the teaching spread throughout the East taking on different characteristics according to the country in which it took root. Although the practices of the Buddhist religion appear so different (Zen, Tibetan, Theravada etc.) the same principle underlies them all: learn to do good; cease to do evil; purify your own mind. A Buddhist has to purify his or her own mind; the Buddha only showed the way. One has to rely on ones' own efforts; Buddhists know of no god or creator that can do the work for them.

Festivals

Buddhist holy days are determined according to the phases of the moon. Instead of a particular day of the week being designated as a holy day, the quarter moon days are used. Lay Buddhists in Western countries try to at least celebrate the full moon day; however, due to the exigencies of their employment generally these days are celebrated on the nearest Sunday.

Each Buddhist school has its own festival days and to enumerate them all is beyond the scope of this publication.

Generally at a feast day the lay supporters will bring food for the participants to share, the monks being fed first followed by the lay supporters. Although vegetarianism is highly regarded, and in some Mahayanan schools compulsory for the monks, this is not universal. Before offering food it is wise to ask what will be acceptable. If one is a vegetarian, asking what is contained in any dish one intends to sample will not cause any offence. A visitor, guest or non-Buddhist would not be expected to offer food unless specifically requested to do so.

Lay Buddhists

Buddhists come from many different cultures and should one be visiting a Buddhist household, the particular customs will, in general, be those of the occupant's racial origins; Eastern, Western, English, Japanese, Thai, ...whatever.

As many Buddhists in the U.K. meditate, some of their time is spent sitting on the floor. Many Western Buddhist families have adopted the Eastern habit of leaving their shoes in the entrance hall of their houses in order to keep their carpets clean enough to sit on, should any one so wish.

Some families have a special room set aside as a shrine room for meditation and study. Should one be invited into this room, shoes should never be worn and it is well to remember that to be invited into such a room is a compliment.

Lay Buddhists do not touch any figurine of the Buddha unless invited to. Although a figurine has no intrinsic religious value it nevertheless represents and is used to focus the mind on the highest values in the Buddhist religion. Therefore any lack of respect to a figure, statue or picture of the Buddha, or even a book containing Buddhist Dhamma (teaching), represents lack of respect to the Buddhist religion.

Monks and Nuns (mendicants)

The relationship between the laity and those mendicants who have 'gone forth' to follow a path of renunciation is mutually supportive. The laity providing the material requisites for the mendicants, which gives them time to focus on the cultivation of the mind; the mendicants in turn providing the spiritual guidance for the laity.

All Theravadin and most Mahayanan mendicants are celibate and any kind of intentional erotic behaviour is forbidden. This includes even suggestive speech, or physical contact with immoral intent. If arranging to meet a Buddhist mendicant it is a good idea to ask if there is anything that needs to be borne in mind to avoid embarrassment. Should one be unexpectedly confronted with a situation involving a Buddhist mendicant, then as long as one acts respectfully and refrains from physically touching him or her, unless contact is initiated by the mendicant, there should be no misunderstandings.

In some schools of Buddhism it is a breach of rules for mendicants to ask for refreshments. It is therefore a kindness to ask if any refreshments are required.

Birth, naming and wedding customs

These ceremonies are very much tied in with the cultural background of the main participants, for example: Western-born Theravadin Buddhists would participate in a different naming ceremony for their children than would Western-born Zen Buddhists; however, they would probably appreciate the same type of presents for their child. To attempt to give advice to cover all exigencies is impractical.

In the various schools of Buddhism the attitude to both the mind and emotions are very similar; however, the outward forms used to express this attitude could vary even from temple to temple within the same school in the same country.

Death customs and funeral rites

Buddhist funeral customs differ according to the country of origin of the deceased. It should be borne in mind that to a Buddhist, death is considered to be a normal inevitable part of life, not surprising or shocking. While it is understood that the bereaved may suffer due to the loss of a loved one, it is recognised that grief helps neither the deceased nor the bereaved; funerals therefore, can be rather matter of fact occasions and very uplifting if the deceased has lived a full, worthwhile, life.

The actual form of the funeral depends again on the school of Buddhism and the ethnic origins of the deceased. It is not practical in this publication to attempt to describe the various procedures.

Diet

Many Buddhists are vegetarian, but it is a personal preference. However, some Mahayanan schools require their mendicants to refrain from eating meat or fish.

Dress

Dress varies according to the customs of the ethnic group represented. When visiting a Buddhist monastery, bear in mind that one may be required to sit on the floor. If there is no way to find out what the arrangements are within the particular establishment it is intended to visit, it is advisable to wear something smart but casual, loose enough to permit one to sit on the floor without stopping one's circulation. Never wear shoes in a Buddhist place of worship.

In the East it would be frowned on for members of either sex to wear shorts into a temple and in most Western establishments this would still apply. Men are expected to at least cover their torso and wear long trousers and women are asked to refrain from wearing any skimpy attire, at least a partial sleeve to the top and skirt to the knee or loose trousers are fine.

Customarily the head is uncovered by both sexes within temples and monasteries; however, if one's custom is to cover the head, as with Sikhs for example, then that is perfectly acceptable.

Main languages spoken

The main language for Buddhists is the spoken language of the country of residence, but depending on the particular school of Buddhism the teachings have been written in either the Pali or Sanskrit language.

Medical treatment

In general the preferences for a Buddhist with regard to medical treatment follow those of the ethnic community to which he or she belongs. There are a few details, however, that should be taken into consideration. It is one of the precepts for many Buddhists that they take no drugs or drink that may cloud the mind. Although the obvious reference is taking substances for recreational use, a Buddhist should be informed of the effects of painkillers and other medicines if they are likely to cause drowsiness or unconsciousness.

Meditation

In all schools of Buddhism meditation is practiced in one form or another. If one is in an area where other people are practising meditation, it is polite to keep as quiet as possible.

Other

In the East a great deal of notice is paid to body language and many Western Buddhists have adopted this attention to body language for very practical reasons. The Buddha's teaching emphasizes awareness. By paying attention to how gestures and movements are used awareness is increased and respect is consciously shown.

Therefore it is not acceptable to stand over mendicants when offering them something or speaking to them but better to try to approach them on the level at which they are sitting.

Buddhists try not to point their feet at a shrine or Buddha image, or lie down in a shrine room.

Buddhists place their hands together in front of the chest with the fingers pointing upwards in the Eastern gesture called "anjali". This is used as a means of greeting and saying goodbye, generally to a mendicant. It is also used as a gesture of respect during a religious service.

Buddhists also prostrate themselves before a shrine and/or a mendicant but would not expect a non-Buddhist to do likewise.

Glossary

As Buddhism spread throughout the East, it came to be expressed in many different languages. Terms in the Sanskrit and Pali of India are in most common use in the West, although Japanese and Tibetan terms also occur frequently. Pali is the language of the texts of the Theravada school, whilst Sanskrit is used for general Mahayana. Zen Buddhism uses terms expressed in Japanese, and Tibetan Buddhism, Tibetan. There is no preferred form.

Pali	Sanskrit	Explanation
	Amitabha Amitayus	Also, Amida (Japanese). Buddhas having unlimited light and life respectively.
Anatta	Anatman	*No self; no soul (trans)*. Insubstantiality; denial of a real or permanent self.
Anicca	Anitya	*Impermanence; transience (trans)*. Instability of all things, including the self.
Arahat, Arahant	Arhat	*Enlightened disciple (trans)*. The fourth and highest stage of Realisation recognised by the Theravada tradition. One whose mind is free from all greed, hatred and ignorance.
Bhikkhu	Bhikshu	Fully ordained Buddhist monk.

Pali	Sanskrit	Explanation
Bhikkhuni	Bhikshuni	Fully ordained Buddhist nun.
Bodhi Tree		The tree *(fiscus religiosa)* under which the Buddha realised Enlightenment. It is known as the tree of Wisdom.
Bodhisatta		*A Wisdom Being (trans)*. One intent on becoming, or destined to become, a Buddha. Gotama, before his Enlightenment as the historical Buddha.
	Bodhisattva	A being destined for Enlightenment, who postpones final attainment of Buddhahood in order to help living beings (see Mahayana).
Brahma Viharas		The four sublime states: loving kindness, compassion, sympathetic joy, and evenness of mind.
Dalai Lama (Tibetan)		*Great Ocean (trans)*. Spiritual and temporal leader of the Tibetan people.
Dana	Dana	*Generosity; giving; gift (trans)*.
Dhamma	Dharma	*Universal law; ultimate truth (trans)*. The teachings of the Buddha. A key Buddhist term.
Dhammapada	Dharmapada	Famous scripture of 423 verses.
Dukkha	Duhkha	*Suffering, ill; unsatisfactoriness; imperfection. (trans)*. The nature of existence according to the first Noble Truth.

Pali	Sanskrit	Explanation
Gompa (Tibetan)		Monastery, place of meditation.
Gotama	Gautama	Family name of the Buddha.
Jhana	Dhyana	Advanced meditation. Also Ch'an (Chinese) and Zen (Japanese).
Kamma	Karma	*Action (trans)*. Intentional actions that affect one's circumstances in this and future lives. The Buddha's insistence that the effect depends on volition marks the Buddhist treatment of kamma as different from the Hindu understanding of karma.
Kesa (Japanese)		The robe of a Buddhist monk, nun or priest.
Lama (Tibetan)		*Teacher (trans)*. One who is revered.
Magga	Marga	*Path (trans)*. Leading to cessation of suffering. The fourth Noble Truth.
	Mahayana	*Great Way* or *Vehicle (trans)*. Teachings that spread from India into Tibet, parts of Asia and the Far East, characterised by the Bodhisattva Ideal and the prominence given to the development of both compassion and wisdom.
Mala		String of 108 beads used in Buddhist practice (like a rosary). Also, Juzu (Japanese).

Pali	Sanskrit	Explanation
Nibbana	Nirvana	*Blowing out* of the fires of greed, hatred and ignorance, and the state of secure perfect peace that follows. A key Buddhist term.
Nirodha	Nirodha	*Cessation* (of suffering). The third Noble Truth.
Sakyamuni	Shakyamuni	*Sage of the Shakyas (trans).* The tribe of the Buddha). Title of the historical Buddha.
Samsara	Samsara	*Everyday life (trans).* The continual round of birth, sickness, old age and death which can be transcended by following the Eightfold Path and Buddhist teaching.
Sangha	Sangha	*Community, assembly (trans).* Often used for the order of bhikkhus and bhikkunis in Theravadin countries. In the Mahayana countries, the Sangha includes lay devotees and priests i.e. Japan.
Satori (Japanese)		*Awakening (trans).* A term used in Zen Buddhism.
Siddattha	Siddhartha	*Wish-fulfilled (trans).* The personal name of the historical Buddha.
Sila	Sila	*Morality (trans).*

Pali	Sanskrit	Explanation
Sutta	Sutra	*Text (trans)*. The word of the Buddha.
Tanha	Trishna	*Thirst; craving; desire (trans)*, (rooted in ignorance). Desire as the cause of suffering. The second Noble Truth.
Tathagata	Tathagata	Another epithet for the Buddha.
Theravada	Sthaviravada	*Way of the elders' (trans.)*. A principal school of Buddhism, established in Sri Lanka and South East Asia. Also found in the West.
Thupa/Cetiya	Stupa	*Reliquary (trans.)*, including Pagodas.
Tulku (Tibetan)		Reincarnated Lama.
Vihara		*Dwelling place; monastery (trans.)*.
Vinaya		The rules of discipline of monastic life.
Vipassana	Vipashyana	Insight into the true nature of things. A particular form of meditation.
Wesak or Vesak (Sinhalese)	Wesak	Buddha Day. Name of a festival and a month. On the full moon of Wesak (in May or June), the birth, Enlightenment and passing away of the Buddha took place, although some schools celebrate only the birth at this time.
Zen		*Meditation (Japanese)*. Derived from the Sanskrit 'dhyana'. A school of Mahayana Buddhism that developed in China and Japan.

References

One of the best sources of general information on subjects pertaining to any Buddhist school is:

The Buddhist Society
58 Eccleston Square
London SW1V 1PH
Tel: 0207 834 5858
www.buddsoc.org.uk

Compiled by Anthony Millett.

Chinese

In many ways the modern Chinese outlook can be traced back to the ancient civilisations of the ChangJiang (Yangtze) and HuangHe (Hwangho) river basins in Central China. Nowadays, when Chinese go to look for their roots they will claim them from here. Those civilisations have, of course, received outside influences over the years with Buddhism, for example, entering China around 65CE. Over the last few hundred years, influences have come from Western nations and after many years of rejection, these influences are now being welcomed. Starbucks and McDonald's restaurants, for example, have opened in Mainland China and global trade continues to grow.

The People's Republic of China (PRC or "mainland" China) represents what most people nowadays think of as China. However, it is to the other three major self-governed Chinese regions – Hong Kong, Singapore, Taiwan – that we should look to understand the communities of "overseas" Chinese (hua qiao or hai wai tong bao). This is because most overseas Chinese – in UK, Europe, US, Canada, Australia and elsewhere – come from (or at least via) these regions.

In the UK, the Chinese community originates mostly from Hong Kong but there are also Chinese from Singapore, Malaysia, Vietnam, Mainland China and elsewhere. In the US there may be a similar mix, but the influence of those from Taiwan may be more evident. Increasingly, though, we find Chinese born in the country of residence. Hence, there are British Born Chinese (BBC), American Born Chinese (ABC) and many other kinds of "resident" born Chinese.

Faith and Belief

| Confucianism |

Confucianism is based on the teachings and writings of the philosopher Confucius (551 – 479BCE). It is an ethical belief system rather than a religion and is based upon the concept of relationships. In Confucianism every relationship – between mother and child, husband and wife, brother and sister – has the dual aspect of responsibility and obligation. However, Confucianism goes beyond the family, and incorporates the relationship of individuals with the state, subject and ruler, bureaucrat and civilian. According to Confucianism, if these responsibilities and obligations are observed then society will be a just and harmonious one.

However, because individuals' roles and boundaries of behaviour were strictly and inflexibly defined, there are continuing conflicts about the role of Confucianism in modern times that still need resolving.

| Daoism |

Daoism (Taoism), like Confucianism, seeks harmony but through a reality beyond the material, that is ultimately beyond name or description. This alternative reality is called the *Dao* (the Way). Harmony is sought between the material and the *Dao*, but it is only achieved through the *Dao*, through natural and spontaneous actions, without set purpose or preference. Daoism is in opposition to Confucianism, in that it encourages action by "gut feeling" rather than by explicit rules or manipulation.

Buddhism

The origins of Buddhism are to be found in India, entering China in the reign of Emperor Han Ming Di in about 65 CE. It did not gain any mass following, though, until around 290 CE. Its popularity arose during a time of social disorder and barbarian invasion. Buddhism's promise of personal salvation, although very much against the norms of Chinese collectivism and emphasis on family and society, attracted many during a time of great uncertainty.

Buddhism was established by Siddhartha Gautama, the Buddha or "enlightened one". Siddhartha Gautama was a prince of the Sakya kingdom on the borders of what are now India and Nepal and was a contemporary of Confucius. Although living in luxury, Siddhartha Gautama was exposed one day to the sufferings of the masses. This greatly affected the prince and he began a search to find relief for human suffering. This he found when he received a moment of enlightenment after which he became the Buddha – the enlightened one.

Buddhism split into two major branches early in its development: Mahayana and Hinayana. The Buddhism of China stems mainly from the former, which incorporates practices like repetitive prayer and belief in re-birth.

Folk Religion

Localised folk religions have been common throughout China, in particular before 1949. Although they have incorporated elements of Buddhism and Taoism, they are often based on local gods. Since ancient times, infused within traditional Chinese belief has been the notion of spirits, in particular those of the dead. Hence, ancestor worship has been a part of folk religion. This is reflected in the popular QingMing festival and in folk customs about birth, marriage and death.

Christianity

Christians have been active in China since the 17th century when Jesuit missionaries of the Roman Catholic Church went to China and when Cossacks serving in the Imperial guard brought Christian Orthodoxy with them. Protestant missionaries first appeared in the early 19th century. By 1949 there were only 3 or 4 million Christians in China, less than 1 percent of the total population. There may be as many as 50 million Christians in China today – still a tiny minority in a country of 1,200 million people – but Christian groups flourish amongst the overseas Chinese.

Other Religions

Islam came to China via the Silk Route, mainly from Central Asia where it was practiced by many of the Turkish peoples. Today there are believed to be about 4 million Chinese Muslims.

Judaism has also been associated with China, through the KaiFung Jews. Their origins (and subsequent disappearance) have been something of a mystery, but it has been reported that several hundred people claimed Jewish ancestry in the 1952 census of ethnic minorities.

Many Chinese are now atheist and agnostic, following the influences of both communism and western capitalism.

Birth, Death and Marriage

Birth

Is traditionally followed by one month of confinement for the mother, after which a celebration takes place. Since boys were traditionally preferred, the celebration might be bigger when a son was born. Naming in Chinese consists of the family name followed by one or two personal names. The name is chosen to have a favourable meaning and to sound pleasant when spoken. One of the two personal names may be shared between brothers or between sisters, or occasionally with cousins: siblings can sometimes be recognised in this way.

Marriage

In China (as elsewhere) used to be arranged. The wife used to live within the husband's extended family and was considered the property of that family. Nowadays, courting is open and free, but often parents get involved introducing marriage customs and tradition once the couple have decided to tie the knot.

As elsewhere, special dress is worn at the wedding, usually red. On the day, the groom visits the bride's house. A ritual of worshipping the ancestors may occur, to be followed by a tea ceremony. Firstly tea is served to the parents by the couple and then it is served to the elder siblings. The couple bow, as a sign of respect, as they serve. Then the couple travels to the groom's house, where the tea ceremony is performed again, after which the bride is considered part of the groom's family. Naturally, a wedding banquet follows.

Traditionally, the wife takes on the family name of the husband, but nowadays the wife may retain her family name.

Death

Is traditionally handled carefully, to enable the souls of the dead to pass peacefully into the afterlife. In Buddhist funerals, replica money (and replicas of other worldly goods) may be burnt so that the dead may take something with them. Traditional, burial locations are chosen with good *feng shui* (e.g. on hillsides with a view) but this is becoming less important. Mourning lasts for 100 days, with black armbands worn by family members. White decorations are worn by the deceased's children and blue by the grandchildren.

Food and Drink

Food is central to the Chinese, in particular to family life. Meal times have been the time for socialising both within the nuclear family and within the extended family. Large banquets are often served at times of celebration (e.g. marriage, New Year) but also as a token of welcome (e.g. for visiting dignitaries and for relatives returning from overseas).

Food and taste is much appreciated in China, in much the same way that wine tasting is appreciated in the West. Food is judged on its colour, bouquet (aroma), flavour and body – the same dimensions that are used for appreciating wine.

Few Chinese dishes have only one ingredient, as this would offer no contrast and therefore no opportunity to harmonise. So usually, there will be a main ingredient and a number of supplementary ingredients. Take pork for example. Its colour is pink and texture tender. It is most likely to be found with a green vegetable, which is either crispy or crunchy such as celery (crunchy) or green peppers (crispy).

Not unexpectedly, tea (a corruption of the Chinese word *cha*) is the main drink in China. It is impossible to go anywhere in China without encountering people drinking tea. Tea is drunk all day – at work, at home, before and after (but not usually during) meals, alone or in company.

Nowadays, the predominance of tea as the major drink is being challenged by popular modern beverages, including coffee and beer. The presence of Starbucks coffee shop in Beijing is a symbol, often mentioned by European and American reporters, of the changing times in that city. Excellent beer has been brewed in China for many decades, in particular in the north eastern provinces.

Festivals

The Chinese New Year

The oldest and most important festival to Chinese people is the Spring Festival, more commonly known in the West as Chinese New Year. Like all traditional Chinese festivals, the date is determined by the Chinese (lunar) calendar, rather than the Western (Gregorian) calendar, so the date of the holiday varies from late January to mid February.

The Spring festival celebrates the earth coming back to life, and the start of ploughing and sowing. In the past, feudal rulers of dynasties placed great importance on this occasion, and ceremonies to usher in the season were performed.

Traditionally, preparations for the New Year festival have started during the last few days of the last moon. Houses are thoroughly cleaned, debts repaid, hair cut and new clothes are bought. Doors are decorated with vertical scrolls, with texts that seek good luck and praise. Incense is burned in temples, and sometimes in homes, as a mark of respect to ancestors.

On New Year's Eve houses are brightly lit and a large family dinner is served. In the south of China sticky-sweet glutinous rice pudding *(nian gao)* is served, while in the north steamed dumplings *(jiao zi)* are popular. Celebrations can last till midnight, when fireworks are lit to drive away evil spirits. New Years day is often spent visiting neighbours, family and friends.

In China the public holiday lasts three days, but the festival traditionally lasts till the 15th day of the lunar month and ends with the 'Lantern Festival'. Houses are decorated with colourful lanterns and a sweet or savoury fried or boiled dumpling made of glutinous rice flour *(yuan xiao)* is eaten.

QingMing Festival

The QingMing festival (meaning "clear light") usually falls on or around 5 April each year. Its origin is in ancestor worship and is traditionally the day when families visit and clean their ancestors' graves. It needn't be a day of sadness – with many tombs in China on mountaintops, it can be an enjoyable walk and picnic for many families.

This is by no means the only day for visits, with some families making regular visits on other days and overseas Chinese making visits to coincide with their trips. It is, however, a commonly recognised day for visits, if not a public holiday.

The Dragon Boat Festival

This festival (DuanYang or DuanWuJie) is a major festival, which takes place on the fifth day of the fifth lunar month, usually in June or July. Dragon Boat races are a feature of this festival, which commemorates the sacrifice and death by drowning of a Chinese poet and high-ranking official, QuYuan. The dragon boats are long and narrow, paddled by teams of men and women to the beat of a drum.

The Mid-Autumn Festival

This festival (ZhongQiu) celebrates the appearance of the full moon and falls on the fifteenth day of the eighth lunar month (usually in September). Moon cakes are eaten during this festival, which consist of egg yolk in almond paste, covered in a rich pastry.

Language

Chinese is one of a small group of languages whose written form does not vary across a wide variety of spoken forms. Hence a Cantonese speaker listening to a Mandarin speaker might not understand anything that was said, but would read with ease the most complex and technical of what was written. There are eight major spoken language groups in China with some 600 dialects. All share the same written form, which nowadays may be written in an abbreviated script.

In total there are over 45,000 Chinese characters; however, a vocabulary of 4,000 would be good and a vocabulary of 9,000 unlikely to anyone without a university degree. All Chinese languages use tones to distinguish different words, with four common tones in PuTongHua (Mandarin), the official national language, and nine (quite different) tones in Cantonese, the language commonly spoken in south eastern China.

Because intonation is part of meaning, it cannot easily be used to express emotion. Take the word "what" in English; disbelief can be inferred within it when a rise tone is added (what!), while the basic meaning remains the same. In Chinese, a change of tone can result in a totally different meaning, so that *mai* can mean buy or sell depending on the tone.

Chinese is also a monosyllabic language, in that each character is no more than a syllable and contains meaning (or at least connotation) independent of characters that precede or follow. With so many meanings and connotations within a given speech or passage of text, this could be confusing, so characters tend to come in pairs. Hence notification of "danger" usually consists of two characters (*wei xian*), both of which mean "danger". Combinations like these clarify meaning.

Medicine

Traditional Chinese Medicine (TCM) is a system of medicine dating back four thousand years. The principles of TCM are based upon the flow of *chi*, a vital force or energy, which, among other things, controls the workings of the human body and mind. *Chi* flows through the body through channels – the 12 'meridians' which correspond to twelve systems such as those of the liver, bladder or spleen. *Chi* may be over- or under-active in a particular system and cause illness. These imbalances can be corrected by a variety of means, the most common being diets and corrective or prophylactic exercises such as "meditation in movement".

There are many ways of diagnosing in TCM, the most important being the pulse (where the energy of the meridians is assessed by the strength, rhythm and quality), the colour of the tongue and the general appearance and demeanour of the person. Thus a patient diagnosed by conventional medicine as having a particular skin disease might be seen as having "excess heat in the liver".

There are a variety of treatments in TCM, including acupuncture and herbal medicine. Acupuncture involves the insertion of extremely fine needles through the skin at particular points along the paths of the meridians in order to balance the chi and stimulate healing. Herbal medicine involves the use of formulae, derived from up to six thousand herbs. There are some standard formulas, but each patient will also be given a unique formula to match his/her unique state and constitution. Herbal medicine has registered a number of spectacular successes in recent years, in particular in the cure of skin diseases. Recently the first Chinese herbal clinic in a National Health Service hospital opened in London.

The continuing practice of TCM does not in any way imply the rejection of Western medicine by Chinese people. Chinese people will in general go to see their general practitioner first, and only resort to TCM when the GP cannot help.

Martial Arts

Despite the name, the Chinese martial arts do not concentrate exclusively on fighting and subduing an opponent. Fundamental to all Chinese martial arts are the concepts of respect, self-discipline, courtesy and inner strength; it is these areas that must be mastered, by the true martial artist.

The popular term for martial arts is *gong fu* (kung fu), but this actually means "great skill". The term that should be used is *wu shu*. *Wu shu* comes in many forms. One famous form originated in the famous ShaoLin Temple of HeNan province. Built in 495 CE in a remote part of the province, the temple was home to Boddhidarma, the founder of Zen. The monks of ShaoLin originally spent the majority of their time in prayer and meditation, an immobile activity, and to counteract stiffness they developed a series of exercises which were modelled on their observations of the natural world – for example the monkey's rapid movements, or the snake's crawling.

Being remote, and often between the spheres of influence of competing warlords, the monks of ShaoLin found that they were often the target of attacks, and so developed their exercises into a form of self defence. Great dedication in training was developed, with body (muscles, flexibility and reflexes) developed alongside the spirit and mind.

Most of the world's martial arts – judo, karate and kendo, for example – trace their origins to *wu shu* including tai ji quan *(tai chi chuan)*. *Tai ji quan* (or just *tai ji*) is an ancient form of gentle movement exercise. It straddles the boundaries between martial arts, exercise and meditation, and can be practiced solo, or in groups. There are many forms of *tai ji*, though all consist of exercises following a precise pattern, learned and refined in concert with a *tai ji* teacher.

Tai ji is graceful both to watch and to perform, and is based on the Daoist philosophy that life is lived most effectively if a person refrains from fighting against the nature. Each movement in tai ji is "created" by its predecessor, so that effort is minimised and so that movement is flowing and liquid. *Tai ji* is therefore "martial" only in the sense that it promotes health and physical well being, that is the basis of any combat activity.

Music and the Performing Arts

Western music and performing arts find equivalents in Chinese form. There are Chinese forms of instruments like the violin *(er hu)* and the flute (bamboo flute), and these may combine to form distinctively Chinese musical groups and orchestras. There are many operatic forms in China, the most famous being the Beijing and the Cantonese.

While Chinese (and even Western) operatic forms are an acquired taste, Chinese music can be more readily appreciated by all. At the recent Oscar ceremonies of the American Academy of Motion Picture Arts and Sciences, the Chinese movie Crouching Tiger, Hidden Dragon won the music award with a modern Chinese score.

Tradition in a Modern World

The latter decades of the 20th century saw spectacular growth in the Asian "tiger" economies, including Hong Kong, Taiwan and Singapore. More recently, those rates of growth have spread to parts of Mainland China. Changing economic structures have inevitably led to cultural change. Just as Britain has left behind many practices of the Victorian period, so China and its people will leave behind some – but not all – of its traditional practices.

Acknowledgements

Special thanks to ChinaTown Online for permission to use material from their website: www.chinatown-online.co.uk in the production of this chapter. This non-political, non-religious and non-partisan site provides information about China, the Chinese community in the UK, Chinese businesses and business involved in trade/commerce with China.

Thanks are also due to:

Portsmouth College

Portsmouth Chinese Association

Portsmouth Chinese School

School of Chinese Language and Culture, Beijing

Mr M Cheung

Mrs L Ma

References

Shi, Su (1994) Elementary Knowledge of Chinese Culture, School of Chinese Language and Culture, Beijing.

Moyse, Sarah (1996) Chinese New Year, Wayland

Tan, Gill (1994) Ethnic Diversity in the Making of Hackney, Hackney Council

The University College of St Martin's Philtar website: www.philtar.ucsm.ac.uk

Compiled by:

George Parks M.B.E
He Guo Zhen
Denis Wong

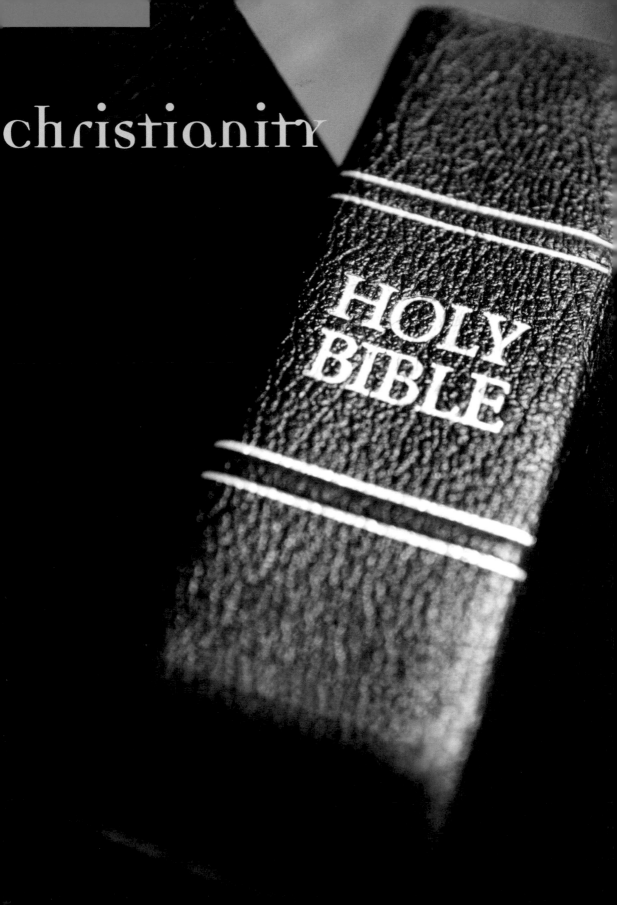

Christianity

A Christian is a follower of Jesus Christ. In the United Kingdom the assumption has been that being British means being Christian. This changed during the second half of the 20th century, partly as a result of people of other faiths becoming British, and partly as a result of modern secularism.

Nonetheless for most British people whose British ancestry goes back for several generations, the lines of cultural identity between "Britishness" and "Christianity" are very closely interwoven. There are, therefore, two general types of Christian in Britain (leaving on one side for the moment the denominational differences): the Christian who positively tries to follow the way of Jesus and to a greater or lesser extent is a church-goer; and the Christian who has a much vaguer idea of what that means, but nonetheless would describe him or herself as a Christian and whose way of life is unconsciously infused with Christian culture and values.

An introduction to the faith

Christianity believes – in common with Judaism and Islam – that there is one God who caused all creation to happen, and that he remains involved with the life of his world. It believes that the world was created good, and that evil and suffering have entered it because of humanity's tendency to turn away from God. It believes that, particularly through his calling of a Chosen People and the witness of many individuals, He continually tried to bring his world back to himself.

Christians also believe that God came down to earth in the person Jesus of Nazareth. Jesus was born to a Jewish family at the beginning of the first millennium.

After what we presume was a normal childhood and the beginnings of a working career, Jesus began a short but extraordinary ministry.

He proclaimed that God's Kingdom had already arrived and was to be found in the way people led their lives: in the qualities of forgiveness, self-denying sacrifice and love. These are the hallmarks of God, and therefore of his Kingdom.

As he travelled round his small country proclaiming this teaching, he gathered a group of disciples and other followers, bringing healing and wholeness to many people. He attracted enthusiastic followers, but he also made enemies. He was arrested and put to death. His followers dispersed, confused and frightened. Then, very quickly, they became convinced that God had brought Jesus back to life. This conviction led them to worship Jesus and they called him Son of God.

They then experienced a surge of divine power that gave them the courage to start telling people about their new conviction, and about what they had seen God do in Jesus. This power they called the Spirit – God at work in them.

Over the next two or three hundred years these convictions were gradually turned into agreed teachings about the nature of God. They wanted to hold on to the Jewish conviction that there is only one God, but they also wanted to do justice to their Christian experiences.

They held these together in what is called the Doctrine of the Trinity – the teaching that the one God is experienced in three distinct ways – as Creator and Father, as the Son, and as the Holy Spirit. These three Natures or Persons are yet One God.

A practising, church-going Christian sees his or her religion involving belief about God's showing of himself in Jesus, belonging to the community of other Christians, and an attempt to behave according to the rules of the kingdom. Jesus summarised those rules as:

Love of God.
Love (meaning care and concern) for others.

These are the golden rules of Christian life-style, and everything else is subordinate to them. They are more like guiding principles therefore many ethical dilemmas today are not precisely legislated for. Churches and individual Christians applying these rules to similar problems may come up with different answers.

There is no clear Christian position on issues such as euthanasia, abortion, nuclear warfare, pacifism or homosexuality to which all denominations adhere. Some denominations will put greater emphasis on the opinion of a central authority; others will rely on the freedom of the individual Christian conscience. All would agree that any proposed answer should be covered by the golden rules.

Almost all Churches will have their main services on Sundays – the day of the week on which the Resurrection happened. A few, e.g. the Seventh Day Adventists, worship on Saturdays – the Old Testament Sabbath day.

Christians are also encouraged to say prayers privately in the morning and at night. The main prayer is called The Lord's Prayer following a pattern Jesus gave to his disciples. Christians living in community together, called monks or nuns, will pray together several times a day.

Denominational Differences

The Christian church had differences of opinion from very early days. These related either to Christian teaching or standards of Christian behaviour or to styles of worship. Gradually the church as a whole developed an orthodox, or commonly agreed, position. Serious divergences from this were called 'heretical'.

As a result of the barbarian invasions in Western Europe and the so-called Dark Ages, the two halves of 'orthodox' Christianity lost touch with each other. They began to develop differently as the Orthodox East and the Catholic West. This resulted in a final split in the year 1201 that has never been reconciled. A number of Eastern Orthodox Christians live in the United Kingdom.

A second split within the Catholic West occurred as a result of the Protestant Reformation in the 16th Century. This led to a number of denominations scattered across Western Europe.

In England and Wales, under King Henry VIII, the church was separated from the authority of Rome, but the teaching and worship remained Catholic. Under his son Edward VI the teaching and worship were turned in a strongly protestant direction. Then under Queen Mary the country returned to Roman authority. Elizabeth I re-established a church separate from Rome and attempted to combine teaching and worship from both Catholic and Protestant traditions. The Church of Scotland adopted the form of Protestantism known as Presbyterian.

The other main Protestant churches in this country are the United Reformed Church (formed from Presbyterians and Congregationalists), churches of the Baptist Union, Methodist churches (which separated from the Church of England in the 18th century) and Pentecostal churches (a movement which has grown in the second half of the 20th century).

Salvationists (founded by William and Catherine Booth in the 19th century) and Quakers (also known as the Religious Society of Friends, established through the work of George Fox in the 17th century) are two denominations, which are acknowledged as having had strong social impact.

Roman Catholics have continued to maintain a presence in this country since the 16th century, and have had an organised church structure since the 19th century.

The twentieth century has seen a substantial growth in the ecumenical movement. This is a process that has sought to bring the Christian denominations closer together.

It is correct to say of any Christian that the religion is Christianity, though the denomination may be Anglican or Roman Catholic or Methodist etc.

Religious Books

The chief religious book for all Christians is The Bible. The word literally means 'Library' and the book is actually a collection of books divided into three sections: the Old Testament, the Apocrypha and the New Testament.

The Old Testament books were written over a period of 800 years by many different people using many different literary styles. Law, legend, history, prophecy, poetry; they all stem from the religious experiences of the people of Ancient Israel who became the Jewish people.

The books of the Apocrypha are from the later period of Israel's history before Christ. Some versions of the Bible include them in the Old Testament whilst others keep them separate.

The books of the New Testament relate to the early Christian period and consist of Gospels (accounts of Jesus' ministry, death and resurrection); one man's version of the story of early church; and letters from early Christian leaders. They date from about 20 years after Jesus' death and the contents were finally fixed in the 4th century. Christians have continued to write and think about aspects of the faith ever since.

Many other works have helped to develop Christian thinking and practice. However the Bible, and particularly the New Testament books, remains the chief inspiration and guide.

Festivals

The main Christian festivals are centred round the key moments of Jesus' life.

Christmas	Celebrates Jesus' birth and God's giving of himself to all humanity, hence the emphasis on the giving of presents. December 25th became the accepted date for this celebration during the 4th century.
Easter	Celebrates Jesus' resurrection from the dead. Christians lead up to it with an annual remembrance of the last week of his life and his death culminating in:

Maundy Thursday – his last meal with his disciples, his betrayal and arrest.

Good Friday – the day of his crucifixion.

Easter Eve – a day of waiting.

Easter Sunday – the day of his resurrection.

The date fluctuates from year to year because the original events took place at the time of the Jewish Passover festival. This was dated according to the moon's cycle. Easter therefore falls on the first Sunday after the first full moon after the Spring Equinox.

Whitsun or Pentecost

Marks the day when the disciples felt the power of the Holy Spirit in them. That came seven weeks after Easter, also on a Jewish festival day.

Other significant religious events

Other dates that relate to the Christian story include Advent, Epiphany and Lent *(see Glossary)*.

There are other annual events which are usually celebrated in Christian churches, but which have an importance for others outside the normal worshipping community:

Harvest Festivals

Celebrate the fruits of creation and usually happen in September or October. Some churches in rural areas may also celebrate other days relating to the agricultural year:

Plough Sunday (January) & Rogation Day (May) ask for God's blessing on the work of the farming industry.

Lammas Day (August) is a thanksgiving like Harvest Festival.

Remembrance Sunday

The Sunday closest to November 11th, remembers those who died in the wars of the 20th Century.

Birth customs and naming ceremonies

A child is given a first name, or 'Christian' name, at birth. It is not uncommon for second, third or more 'Christian' names to also be given to the child. These precede the 'surname' or 'family' name.

In almost all Christian denominations, a new Christian is made a member of the church's community by Baptism. Where the new Christian is a baby or young child, the declarations about faith and following the Christian way are made by those who bring the child to be baptised – parents and godparents. Baptism is often also called Christening after the white robe babies were traditionally dressed in for their baptism. At Baptism the child's given names are formalised in the eyes of God.

Death customs and funeral rites

Funerals normally take place within a week or two of a death. Christians may be either buried or cremated. A burial would normally be preceded by a service in church. A cremation may sometimes be preceded by a church service; frequently however the cremation is followed by a later service in church and the burial of ashes.

A Christian funeral service combines thanksgiving for the life of the deceased with prayer for those who grieve and a commendation of the deceased into God's everlasting mercy. Black is no longer worn exclusively, but clothing would normally keep a sombre note. A Memorial Service may follow some months after a death. The purpose will be to give thanks for the deceased's life in a more public context.

Diet

There are no food prohibitions, though Christians in some traditions will voluntarily abstain from eating certain things at certain times – in Lent or on Fridays when some Christians do not eat meat. In some traditions, the drinking of alcohol is discouraged.

Dress

Until relatively recently, people attending church would dress in 'Sunday best'. Except on special occasions this has now changed. Women will sometimes wear hats; men should never wear hats inside a church.

The giving of gifts

Gifts in general	Flowers are always acceptable.
Gifts for a newborn child	Congratulations cards are available from many outlets. Flower arrangements and baby clothes are appropriate.
Gifts at Baptism	Traditionally, presents at a Baptism would only be expected from godparents or close relatives although it is not unusual for other guests to also bring gifts.
Wedding gifts	People invited to attend marriages would be expected to bring a present. Often the bride and groom will arrange to leave a list of suggested gifts with a department store of their choice from which guests invited to the wedding can make their selection.

Main languages spoken

All across the world, Christians mostly use their native language for worship and for religious study. Until recently the Western Roman Catholic Church used Latin as the main language for worship. In the Orthodox East, Greek was used in a similar way.

In some developing countries, Christians will use the language in which Christianity was brought to them. In the Church of England, most churches worship in Modern English, but many churches will have some services using the language of the 17th century Prayer Book; a few churches will only use the 17th century book.

Marriage

Marriage is seen by Christians to be part of God's intention for all mankind. The Bible shows that Jesus considered marriage to be a life-long commitment. Many Christians have therefore considered the remarriage of divorcees in church to be wrong. Others have placed greater emphasis on Jesus' command to forgive. Different denominations, and even different clergy within the same denomination, will make different responses. Many clergy who will not re-marry in church may nonetheless offer a service after a civil wedding that both offers a second chance and yet also makes a distinction.

Traditionally a wife takes her husband's surname on marriage although increasingly women are in favour of retaining their own surnames after marriage.

Medical treatment

A few Christian denominations have reservations about blood transfusions, but most think that life-enhancing medical treatment is right. Serious reservations are emerging about genetic cloning, however.

Glossary

Unlike some of the glossaries in other chapters of this guide, most of the terms given below are in English and will be familiar to many people. The historic languages of the Christian scriptures are Hebrew, Greek and Latin. The Old Testament was written largely in Hebrew, with some texts in Aramaic and Greek (Acrocrypha). The whole of the Old Testament was translated into Greek, although many words and passages have their origin in Aramaic. The New Testament was first written in Greek. Latin became increasingly the language of the Western Church from the 5th century AD when the Bible was translated into Latin.

Preferred Form	Main Variants	Explanation
AD	Anno Domini	*In the Year of our Lord (trans).* The Christian calendar dates from the estimated date of the birth of Jesus Christ. Known as CE (Common Era) by other faith communities.
Advent		*Coming (trans).* The period beginning on the fourth Sunday before Christmas (40 days before Christmas in the Eastern Orthodox tradition). A time of spiritual preparation for Christmas.
Altar	Communion Table Holy Table	Table used for Eucharist, Mass, Lord's Supper.
BC	Before Christ	Period of history before the estimated birth of Jesus Christ. Known as BCE (Before the Common Era) by other faith communities.
Baptism	Christening	Rite of initiation involving immersion in, with sprinkling or pouring of, water.

Preferred Form	Main Variants	Explanation
Christ	Messiah	*The anointed one (trans)*. Messiah is used in the Jewish tradition to refer to the expected leader sent by God, who will bring salvation to God's people. Jesus' followers applied this title to him, and its Greek equivalent, Christ, is the source of the words Christian and Christianity.
Christmas		Festival commemorating the birth of Jesus Christ (25 December in most Churches).
Church		(i) The whole community of Christians. (ii) The building in which Christians worship (iii) a particular denomination.
Easter		Central Christian festival that celebrates the resurrection of Jesus Christ from the dead.
Epiphany		January 6th. Marks the coming of the Wise Men to Bethlehem after Jesus' birth. In some parts of the Eastern Church this is kept as Christmas.

Preferred Form	Main Variants	Explanation
Eucharist		*Thanksgiving (trans)*. A service celebrating the sacrificial death and resurrection of Jesus Christ, using elements of bread and wine *(see Holy Communion)*.
Godparents		Should themselves be members of the Christian community. They undertake both a spiritual responsibility for the child's growth in the faith, and usually a social responsibility for the child's general welfare.
Heaven		The place, or state, in which souls will be united with God after death.
Hell		The place, or state, in which souls will be separated from God after death.
Holy Communion		Central liturgical service observed by most Churches. Recalls the last meal of Jesus, and celebrates his sacrificial and saving death.
Holy Spirit		The third person of the Holy Trinity. Active as a divine presence and power in the world, and in dwelling in believers to make them like Christ and empower them to do God's will.

Preferred Form	Main Variants	Explanation
Jesus Christ		The central figure of Christian history and devotion. The second person of the Trinity.
Lent		Penitential season. The 40 days leading up to Easter.
Mass		Term for the Eucharist, used by Roman Catholics and other Churches.
Trinity		The three persons in one God: doctrine of the three-fold nature of God – Father, Son and Holy Spirit.

Compiled by Canon Jonathan Meyrick

Hinduism

Faith/Culture

The word 'Hinduism' is a collective term for the religious beliefs and practices of the Hindus, although it is not generally used by them. They call it *Sanatana dharma* – the eternal cosmic order, and distinguish it from *Brahmanisn*[1] or *Vedic Dharma*, which is essentially monotheistic, and that part of the religion that has come from the early Indo-European times. The authoritative basis for Hinduism are the *Vedas*[2] (knowledge), literature that was allegedly brought into the Indian subcontinent. Hinduism is characterised by not having a founder.[3]

The terms 'Hindu' and 'Hinduism' were coined by nations outside of India to designate the people and religion of the country to the east of the River Sindhu or Indus. Ironically, the River Indus after which India is named is now in Pakistan.

Modern Hinduism, as practised today, probably goes back to between fifteen hundred and a thousand years. Actively promoted at the time presumably to stem the popularity of other religions such as Buddhism, Islam and Christianity.

Hinduism is not evangelical and one must be born a Hindu to be one – although recent reform movements allow the possibility.

Main languages spoken

Whilst Hinduism stems from India and acknowledges its Vedic origins, it has evolved as it moved with Hindu people to various parts of the world including Britain, South East Asia, Nepal, Africa and North America. India itself has something like 16 major languages and an estimated

[1] The word Brahmanism pertains to Brahman – the absolute entity which is the ultimate reality in Hinduism, and should not be confused with Brahmin – a man of the Brahmin caste, one of the four heredity castes, or Brahma, who with Vishnu and Shiva are depicted as the three aspects of God. See also a description of the caste system under 'Other.'

[2] The Vedas (four in all) were composed in a language similar to old Persian. They pre-date the Indo-European venture into the Indian subcontinent. In it society had a high ethics and culture. Science was a central concern and technology pursued. These were the people that produced the Iron Age.

[3] See A Simple Guide to Hinduism, Global Books Limited 1997, for a more comprehensive treatment of the subject.

79

874 regional dialects. The official Indian languages are: Hindi, Urdu, Bengali, Marathi, Gujarathi, Oriya, Assamese, Punjabi, Tamil, Telegu, Malyalam, Karnataka, Konkini, Kashmiri, Sindhi and Sanskrit plus English. Hindus in this country will speak one or more of the above languages depending on their place of origin. The religious language is Sanskrit.

An introduction to the faith

Hindus believe in an indescribable, all encompassing oneness, an ultimate reality, referred to as Brahman, which English speaking people would call God. However when it comes to conceptualising it, it takes on many forms with attributes. Brahman is depicted as having three aspects – Brahma – the creator, Vishnu – the sustainer and Mahesh – the completer. Hindus conceive God in many forms depending on the specific traditions of individuals from different geographical locations. For example, Mahesh is also called Shiva. The female aspect is not forgotten and Shiva's female complement is called Shakti who has given rise to mother goddesses and female cults. She is also known as Kali and Durga. Vishnu is fully manifested (also known as an avatar) as Krishna, the dark god, and the great appeal of Hanuman – the monkey god is a recognition of the ultimate oneness.

A central belief is in the existence of a cosmic or natural order, a balanced way of living, physically, socially, ethically and spiritually. These are interpreted as the four human achievements: Dharma – cosmic order which is maintained by righteousness and observing social and religious law,

Artha – acceptance of wealth, possession and power, the creation of a sustainable society. Kama – achieving quality and enjoyment of life in a balanced way, not to be confused with hedonism. Moksha – the ultimate goal, liberation from the cycle of births and deaths. Fundamental to the notion of Dharma is a duty to others and the requirement to be responsible for one's actions, failure to do so results in a price to pay and this is called karma. However life is enduring and if something does not arise here and now it will manifest itself in reincarnation.

There are three plus one stages in life. These are: brahmachari – a student, grihastha – a householder, vanaprastha – one who has retired from active life and starts to give back to society. Sannyasin – a person who has renounced worldly things is the fourth stage.

Festivals

Living in harmony with the cosmos is one of the main tenets of Hinduism and astrology is part of the ongoing approach to ecological time. Festivals are used to structure the year and express oneself in meaningful thought. There are cultural and geographical differences and not everyone celebrates the same festival.

Holi

The festival Holi is held on the last full moon day at the beginning of Spring. It is a fresh start transcending barriers. Members of all classes (and often from other religions) and sexes mingle, sprinkling one another with cascades of coloured powders and liquids. It is a day when grievances are forgotten. People embrace each other and get together to eat, drink, sing and dance.

| Divali | A family festival of lights in late October/early November, symbolising the victory of righteousness and the lifting of spiritual darkness. The word Divali literally means rows of diyas (oil lamps made of clay). It celebrates the family as a microcosm of the universe, where men and women have equality of status, with each playing to their own strengths. Family, relatives and friends gather to offer prayers, celebrate and distribute sweets to the less fortunate. |

Other significant religious events

| Akhand Path | The major epics are sometimes recited uninterruptedly over a period of days to mark a significant event or as a gesture of thanksgiving. |
| Tirtha Yatra | Pilgrimages are an essential aspect of Hinduism and are undertaken periodically. Reasons vary, from taking the ashes of ancestors to be submerged in the holy River Ganges or in order to ask for a boon in fulfilment of some desire. |

Festivals need not always be dedicated to a god or goddess. The delightful festival of Raksha (protection) Bandhan (to tie) for example is held in August. Girls and married women tie a rakhi – made from a twisted gold or yellow and red thread on the right wrist of their brother and feed him with Indian sweets. He in turn promises to protect his sister and gives her a gift in return. Sometimes the gesture is extended to a brother-in-law and if the brother happens to be out of town, the rakhi arrives by post.

There are different stories about the origins of Raksha Bandhan. But one charming story relates how a Hindu queen, Padmini, sought protection from the Mughal Emperor by sending him a rakhi after she was threatened by a minor Muslim king. The Emperor respected the rakhi and defended the honour of Padmini. In the same way, even today, a rakhi in Hindu communities all over the world is usually honoured, even when the recipient is not a Hindu.

Diet

The importance of a good diet, its effects on the body and the hygiene requirements for proper preparation is well accepted although interpreted ritualistically. A central belief is that 'a healthy diet produces a healthy body and a healthy body produces a healthy mind'.

Food is categorised according to its effects. These are described as three gunas[4] (properties). Firstly, sattvic foods which are generally light and nutritious. This group consists of dairy products, some legumes, cereals, fruits and vegetables, but little or no spices. Rajasic foods are those that cause heat and stimulation in the body. They include the same food groups and the difference lies mainly in the liberal use of spices and herbs in their preparation. The third kind of foods, the tamasic group, also includes fish and meat. Such food is characterised by hot, spicy, bitter and fermented foods, which have a dulling effect. Stale or foods past their use-by date are considered tamasic. Many Hindus practice vegetarianism as a mark of respect for all life, however it is not universal. The diet of the Vedic

[4] It is believed that all phenomena are composed of gunas. For example these properties can be applied to food as here, or people.

people, which included fish, meat, cereals, fruit, vegetables, dairy products and liquor is still enjoyed by many. Even in families where meat is eaten quite often the women of the house are vegetarians.

All Hindus generally avoid beef, as the cow is considered sacred. Traditional families, particularly Brahmins, prefer to remain vegetarian and will avoid onion, garlic and alcohol. Food prepared for use in temples must not be polluted by these ingredients. The cook must not taste the food after cooking, as that would make it impure. Generally food is offered to the gods before it is consumed.

Customs and courtesies

Hindus generally greet each other and say goodbye with palms held together as if saying prayers, and say 'Namaste' – which literally means – 'I recognise the god in you'.

Traditional concepts of purity and pollution may be rejected by intellectual Hindus but are adhered to unconsciously. Anything other than fresh water for cleansing is considered unhygienic. For example, the Hindu as a rule, in India anyway, does not use toilet paper, and even when it is used, the left hand and water are used to complete cleansing. Therefore even though hands are scrupulously cleaned with soap and water the left hand is considered impure. Food must only be eaten with the right hand, and if given a gift, elders might well insist that it be accepted in the right hand.

Gifts of fruits and flowers are generally acceptable both in the place of worship and by Hindus themselves. For everything else it is wise to check with your acquaintance, as Hindu customs are so very diverse.

Medical treatment

Hindus have no problems accepting medical treatment as they respect life and health. In India there is a history of sophisticated indigenous Ayurvedic medicine going back at least two thousand years. It distinguishes between environmental, organic and psychosomatic causes. It is holistic, contextual and recognises that different medicines serve different purposes and flourishes side by side with modern Western medicine.

Birth customs

Hinduism is a way of life and everything evolves around scripture-based rites. These are very specific and include details on prayers and various preparations to suit every occasion. Children are important, particularly sons to perpetuate the family and necessary to perform the funeral rites for ancestors. Rites associated with the birth of a child include:

Garbhadana	A ceremony performed as a thanksgiving after a woman has conceived.
Jatakarma	After childbirth to welcome the child into the family and thanksgiving for the health of both the mother and child.
Annaprasana	Celebrated when the first solid food, rice cooked in milk, is given to the child when it is six months old.

Rites associated with the first haircut or mundan, introduction to formal education and puberty are also important.

Names and naming ceremonies

Namakarna

The rite of naming the child is usually carried out by the family priest on the 11th day after the birth according to the horoscope. Names are generally suggestive of divine qualities of the vedic deities.

No more than a name is sufficient to put anybody in his or her place. And that place is never, as it is supposed to be in the West, designed for the personality of a single individual. It positions the individual in a specific community whose attributes are assumed in advance. So for example, the family name of a Brahmin might be Divedi – this would mean they were from a community where two Vedas, or Trivedi – where three Vedas, or Chaturvedi – where four Vedas, were studied. Certain groups have an intricate system consisting of a personal name, and initials denoting the name of the ancestral village and father.

Situated in a family a person is at the hub and intimately aware of relationships which are made specific with an elaborated set of names. For example – Dada – Paternal grandfather, Dadi – paternal grandmother, Nana – maternal grandfather, Nani – maternal grandmother, Chacha – father's younger brother, chachi – his wife;

Taya – father's older brother, Tayi – his wife. Devar – husband's younger brother, Devarani – his wife and the list goes on.

Death customs and funeral rites

Death is seen as liberation and the bodies of Hindus are generally cremated. After being ritually bathed the body is placed on an open wooden pyre[5] facing either north or south. After some scriptural chants and worship rituals, the eldest son (or other relative) lights some kindling and walks around the pyre chanting a prayer for the well being of the departed soul before lighting the pyre. If possible, ashes are sprinkled into a holy river such as the Ganges. Hindus carry Ganges water around the world because it should be the last thing that is put into the mouth when a Hindu dies. Dead ancestors are remembered with respect and yearly offerings include a mixture of rice and sesame seeds offered by the eldest male child.

Dress code

Women are generally dressed modestly, and even modern young Hindu women would rather wear trousers or a long skirt, particularly on traditional occasions. Hinduism is communal rather than congregational and people come together to worship in temples – mandir. One is expected to remove shoes and leave them outside before entering. Men, and particularly women, keep their heads covered whilst offering prayers.

[5] In India, however in this country and increasingly in India, crematoria are used.

Literature

Apart from the Veda, which seek to reveal the mystery of the universe with an incomparable richness and diversity, Hinduism has a vast collection of literature spanning many centuries. They contain practical summaries of Hinduism and feature specialised traditions of learning. They provide instructions for the proper pursuit of living including religious law, government, economics and the conduct of domestic ceremonies (marriage and funeral rituals) etc. The two major epics which dominate are:

Ramayana	Its surviving text runs to 24,000 couplets celebrating the birth, education and adventures of Rama, the ideal man and king and his ideal wife Sita.
Mahabharata	This vast work of early Indian literature, running to 100,000 couplets, relates the struggle between two families. It also incorporates a mass of other romantic, legendary, philosophic and religious material. It includes the Bhagavad Gita – The Lord's Song, probably Hinduism's most important single text.

Other

Much of the adaptive development of Hinduism was crystallised in a hereditary caste system. The word 'caste' comes from the Portuguese and the correct term is varna (societal groupings). These are kshatriya – kings, warriors and technologists; brahmin – historians, educators, priests and vaishya – agriculturists and artisans, (now extended to include traders of goods and finance), Shudras – those that served. They were not originally hereditary. Nor were there any rules limiting social interaction or marriage between these classes. Traditional Hindus observe these divisions even today all around the world.

At its core, Hinduism is one of the greatest and most profound 'religions' of the world, but there is a huge gap which separates its highest spiritual understanding from localised superstitious practices. It is hoped that the reader will continue the journey of discovery to deepen their understanding of Hinduism from where the above brief account must leave off.

Glossary

The main references are to Sanskrit terminology, although variants are found and used in other Indian languages. Lakshmi, Laksmi, Vishnu or Vis Visnu type variants are not always included because of their frequency. Many of these terms will also be found in books on Buddhism and Sikhism, but with somewhat different meanings.

Preferred Form	Main Variants	Explanation
Akhand Path		Uninterrupted recitation
Annaprasana		Celebrated when the first solid food is given to a child
Artha		Economic development. The second aim of life

Preferred Form	Main Variants	Explanation
Avatar	Avatara Avtara	*One who descends (trans).* Refers to the descent of a deity, most commonly Vishnu. Sometimes it is translated as *incarnation* which, although inaccurate, may be the best English word available.
Ayurvedic		Ancient indigenous medicine
BCE		Before the Common Era. Equivalent to BC in Christianity.
Bhagavad Gita	Bhagwad Gita	*The Song of the Lord (trans).* Spoken by Krishna, this is the most important scripture for most Hindus. Tradition dates it back to 3,000 years BCE, though most scholars attribute it to the first millennium BCE. Considered an Upanishad.
Brahma		A Hindu deity, considered one of the Trimuti, and in charge of creative power; not to be confused with Brahman or Brahmin.
Brahmachari	Brahmacari Brahmacharin Brahmacarin	One in the first stage of life. A celibate student of Vedic knowledge.
Brahman		The ultimate reality, all the all-pervading reality; that from which everything emanates, in which it rests and into which it is ultimately dissolved.

Preferred Form	Main Variants	Explanation
Brahmin	Brahman Brahmana	The first of the four varnas, the principal social groupings from which priests are drawn. Some writers, rather confusingly, use the spelling 'brahman', and the meaning only becomes clear in the context of a few sentences (see also Brahman and Brahma).
CE		Common Era. Equivalent of AD in Christianity.
Dharma		*Religion or religious duty* is the usual translation into English, but literally it means *the intrinsic quality of the self or that which sustains one's existence*.
Dhoti		A garment made of natural fibre (usually cotton or silk), worn by males, which covers the lower body and legs.
Divali	Diwali Dipavali Deepavali calendar.	Festival of lights at the end of one year and the beginning of the new year, according to one Hindu
Durga		Female deity. A form of the goddess Parvati; wife of Shiva.
Ganesha	Ganesh Ganapati Ganaputi	A Hindu deity portrayed with an elephant's head – a sign of strength. The deity who removes obstacles.

Preferred Form	Main Variants	Explanation
Ganga		*The Ganges (trans)*. Most famous of all the sacred rivers of India.
Grihastha	Gristhi Grhastha	The second stage of Hindu life; one who belongs to that stage, i.e. the householder (grihasti).
Guna		*Rope; quality (trans)*. Specifically refers to the three qualities of sattva (goodness), rajas (passion) and tamas (ignorance), which permeate and control matter.
Guru		Spiritual teacher, preceptor or enlightener.
Hanuman		The monkey warrior who faithfully served Rama and Sita. Also called Pavansuta – *son of the wind of God (trans)*.
Holi		The festival of colours, celebrated in Spring.
Kali	Kaali	Name given to that power of God which delivers justice – often represented by the Goddess Kali (a form of Durga).
Kali yuga		The fourth of the ages; the iron age or the age of quarrelling and hypocrisy.
Kama		The third of the four aims of life – regulated sense of enjoyment.

Preferred Form	Main Variants	Explanation
Karma		*Action (trans)*. Used of work to refer to the law of cause and effect.
Kirtan		Songs of praise; corporate devotional singing, usually accompanied by musical instruments.
Krishna		Usually considered an avatar of Vishnu. One of the most popular of all Hindu deities in contemporary Britain.
Kshatriya	Khatri	Second of the four varnas of traditional Hindu society, the ruling or warrior class.
Mahabharata		The Hindu epic that relates the story of the five Pandava princes. It includes the Bhagavad Gita.
Mahesh		The completer, one of the Hindu trinity.
Mandir		*Temple (trans)*.
Mantra		That which delivers the mind. Refers to a short sacred text or prayer, often repeated repetitiously.
Moksha	Moksa	Ultimate liberation from the process of transmigration, the continuous cycle of birth and death.
Mundan		The head-shaving ceremony. Performed in the first or third year of life.

Preferred Form	Main Variants	Explanation
Murti	Moorti	*Form (trans)*. The image or deity used as a focus of worship. 'Idol' should definitely not be used, and 'statue' may also cause offence.
Namaste		A greeting that literally means 'I recognise the god in you'.
Nirvana		The cessation of material existence.
Parvati		The consort of Shiva, also known by other names such as Durga, Devi etc.
Prashad	Prasad Prasada Prashada	Sacred or sanctified food.
Puja	Pooja	*Worship (trans)*. A general term referring to a variety of practices in the home or mandir.
Rama		The incarnation of the Lord, and hero of the Ramayana (avoid using the variant 'Ram' for obvious reasons.
Ramayana	Ramayan	The Hindu epic that relates to the story of Rama and Sita, composed by the sage Valmiki thousands of years ago.
Sadhu	Saddhu	Holy man, ascetic.

Preferred Form	Main Variants	Explanation
Sannyasin	Samyasin Samnyasin	A renunciate who, having given up worldly affairs and attachments, has entered the fourth stage of life, often as a mendicant.
Sanskrit		Sacred language of the Hindu scriptures.
Shakti	Sakti	Energy or power, especially of a Hindu feminine deity.
Shiva	Siva (many variants, even Civa, have been found)	A Hindu god. The name means *Kindly (trans)*. or auspicious.
Sita	Seeta	The divine consort of Rama.
Swastika	Svastika	From the Sanskrit for well-being; a mark of good fortune. The four arms signify the four directions (space), the four Vedas (knowledge), and the four stages (time) in the life cycle. Not to be confused with the Nazi symbol.
Trimurti		*The Three Deities (trans)*. Refers to Brahma, Vishnu and Shiva, who personify and control the three gunas. They represent and control the three functions of creation, preservation and destruction. "Trinity" should be avoided.

Preferred Form	Main Variants	Explanation
Upanishad	Upanisad	*To sit down near (trans)*. A sacred text based on the teaching of a guru to a disciple. The Upanishads explain the teachings of the Vedas.
Vanaprastha		The third stage of life, typified by retirement and asceticism.
Varna		*Colour (trans)*. The four principal divisions of Hindu society. It is important to note that the word 'caste' refers strictly to sub-divisions within each varna, not to varnas themselves.
Vishnu	Visnu	A Hindu god. With Brahma and Shiva forms the Trimurti.
Yatra	Jatra	*Pilgrimage (trans)*. Usually to important sacred places in India.

References/further reading

Venika Kingsland, (1997) *Simple Guide to Hinduism*, Global Books Ltd.

Venika Kingsland, (1999) *Simple Guide to India: Customs & Etiquette*, Global Books Ltd. 2nd ed.

Romila Thapar, (1990) *A History of India, Volume One*, Penguin

Percival Spear, (1990) *A History of India, Volume Two*, Penguin

Karel Werner, (1994) *A Popular Dictionary of Hinduism*, Curzon Press

Kamala Subramaniam, (1988) *Mahabharata*, Bharata Vidya Bhavan

N.Raghunathan, (1981) *Shrimad Valmiki Ramayana*, Vighneshwar

S. Radhakrishnan, (1953) *The Principal Upanishads*, George Allen & Unwin

Raimundo Pannikar, (1977) *The Vedic Experience*, University of California Press

A.L.Basham, (1959) *The Wonder That Was India*, New York

Swami Venkatesananda, (1989) *The Concise Srimad Bhagavatam*, State University of New York Press

Compiled by Venika Mehra Kingsland

islam

Islam

This Arabic 'logo type' is composed of the words 'Salla-llahu alaihi was sallam' – peace and blessings of Allah upon him. They are used every time the Prophet Muhammad ﷺ is mentioned. Similar respect is accorded to the other Prophets. Alternatively the phrase 'peace be upon him' (pbuh) may be used as can be seen in this chapter.

The religion of Islam is based on the revelations given to the Prophet Muhammad (pbuh) in Arabia during the seventh century CE.

An introduction to the faith

Islam means 'submission to the will of Allah'. Its creed – "There No God but Allah and the Prophet Muhammad (pbuh) is His Messenger" – decrees twin absolutes; i.e. Allah, as One and only Creator, with no family or partners and Muhammad (pbuh) as his last and final prophet and true messenger.

Belief in Allah makes it obligatory on Muslims also to believe in:

All His Prophets – from Adam to Jesus then Muhammad (pbuh).

All His Four Books – the Torah, Zabur, Enjeel (Bible) and the Qur'an.

All His Angels & Jinns.

In life after death and in the day of judgement.

Belief in the Prophet Muhammad (pbuh) makes it obligatory on Muslims to believe in his finality and on his Tradition, i.e. his Sunnah – his pronouncements, his interpretations of the Qur'an, his practices and the examples he set, as well as Supremacy of the Divine Will and predestination.

Muslim culture is based on the above faith.

Islam insists on total equality of nations and races. The indigenous culture of people living in different geographic regions of the Muslim world can only be preserved in the overall framework of Islam. There is just as much affinity between the Muslims of the west coast of America and those of the east coast of China as there is diversity.

The famous five pillars of Islam are the foundation of belief and practices in Islam as much as they are the arch stones of its culture. They are:

The Shahadah	The declaration of faith, which consists of the statement. 'There is no god except Allah, Muhammad (pbuh) is the Messenger of Allah'.
The Salah	Prayers, five times a day, based on the timing of the sun in a locality.
The Sawm	Fasting – obligatory in the month of Ramadan, otherwise voluntary.
The Zakah	Giving a percentage value of unused assets (money, jewellery, land etc.) in charity each year to the deserving, so that it reaches the needy individual rather going than to a group of people or to an institution.
The Hajj	Pilgrimage to Makkah (Mecca) once in a lifetime.

All the above are obligatory to every Muslim (with minor exceptions) except that the Zakah and Hajj are only obligatory to those who can afford them.

Hence Islam is a society of people in prayer. Salah is offered five times a day either at home or in a local mosque, on Fridays in the central mosque of a locality or township, twice a year on the festival days of two Ids in stadium-type enclosures in big cities and finally, once in a lifetime in the pilgrimage at Makkah.

Islamic belief is that all creatures and humans are born Muslims. Also, that a Muslim is in a state of 'prayer' throughout his or her life. This explains why a Muslim's life is lead in complete submission to the will of Allah. A Muslim must live a clean and pious life but not as a hermit. He must live it according to the Sunnah – model practices, customs and traditions of the Prophet Muhammad (pbuh).

Significant religious events

There are no festivals in Islam, only thanks-giving prayers, as Islam forbids demonstrative 'festivity' and processions etc. Neither are there birthday celebrations of any prophet or apostle in Islam. However, some Muslims do interpret this less literally and may regard some important days, such as Id as festivals, such as important days in other faiths are celebrated.

In The Mosque

All religious prayers are strictly separate gender affairs because the postures of Salah are different for men and women. The rule of segregation is based on the principle of Mehram – Na Mehram (close relative – stranger) as well as immense respect to women. Mehram is the one with whom a girl or woman is most closely related, e.g. her husband, father, brother, grandparents, etc, with whom she cannot enter into marriage. All others, including first cousins, uncles, and the in-laws etc are Na Mehrams. A Muslim woman must observe purdah or wear a hijab (scarf) in front of a Na Mehram. Most Muslim gatherings are segregated (in Muslim countries even airports have segregated entry points though this rule is observed less and less).

Women have their own area of the mosque in which to pray. If they join in with the general congregation they must be right at the back so that men do not see them posturing etc. The only relaxation to this rule is at the Ka'bah itself (the main mosque in Makkah) where men and women are allowed to mix. Shoes are not worn in mosques or on places where prayers take place, such as prayer mats. This is to ensure that such places remain clean for the postures of Salah, which include touching the ground with the forehead. If a disability prevents a Muslim from praying in the accepted style then he or she is permitted to pray sitting on a chair.

Birth customs & naming ceremonies

Marriages within 'The People of the Book' (Muslims, Jews and Christians) are permissible, as long as they are practising. The laws of Islam state that every child is born as a Muslim (as are all creatures). The family line starts from the male and if a Muslim woman marries a Christian or a Jew, then any children from the union must be brought up as Muslims. It is the duty of both parents to bring up a child in Islam, even if only one of them is a Muslim.

The luxury of 'let the child choose' is not affordable in Islam as the child will not be able to exercise that choice till adulthood and he or she cannot be left to lead a non-religious life until then.

At birth the adhan (call to prayer) is said in the baby's ears. The baby's head is normally shaved on the seventh day. It is Sunnah to sacrifice a halal animal but it is not obligatory. However, if this is done then the meat should be distributed among the relatives and the poor. Muslim residents in the West usually send money to their native lands or to other Muslim countries where there is a need.

The naming of the child traditionally happens at the moment of the sacrifice and it is the duty of the parents to give the child a proper and meaningful name. Male children are circumcised as soon as possible. The naming and sacrificial ceremony is called the Aqiqah.

When the child is able to recognise the alphabet he or she begins formal learning with a ceremony called Bismillah when the child recites the first Qur'anic verse: "Begin in the name of Allah, the most Beneficent, the most Merciful". This ceremony can be performed in a social gathering anywhere, preferably in a mosque.

Birth outside Islamic marriage is a cardinal sin. There can never be a marriage between a Muslim and any other religion, other than Christianity and Judaism. There cannot be a marriage with a non-believer either. Co-habitation and adultery are haram (forbidden) and both are capital crimes in Islamic countries and punishable by death by stoning. However, Muslims are advised to abide by the laws of the land if they are living in a non-Islamic country.

Death customs and funeral rites

Death brings out (or should bring about) the best of all the grace the occasion demands in Islam. It is treated as the start of real life – the eternal life. Mourning is allowed only as long as it is full of prayers and with no audible crying. It is paramount that the body is cleansed, bathed, prepared and buried immediately. One should not even wait for the arrival of the closest of relatives if they cannot arrive in time. It is, therefore, possible to bury a father without the son present. The coffin is only an unstitched white shroud.

On the death of the wife the marriage is instantly terminated and the husband becomes a Na Mehram (as explained earlier) which means he is no longer allowed to see his wife's face, even in death. This is to ensure respect for the deceased. Kissing the deceased is not permitted.

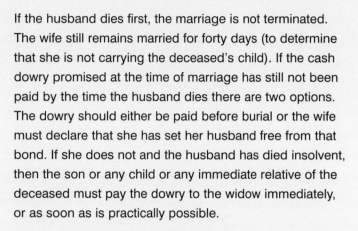

If the husband dies first, the marriage is not terminated. The wife still remains married for forty days (to determine that she is not carrying the deceased's child). If the cash dowry promised at the time of marriage has still not been paid by the time the husband dies there are two options. The dowry should either be paid before burial or the wife must declare that she has set her husband free from that bond. If she does not and the husband has died insolvent, then the son or any child or any immediate relative of the deceased must pay the dowry to the widow immediately, or as soon as is practically possible.

There are traditionally no mourning days, remembrance days or anniversaries for someone who has died.

Diet

Muslims, like Jews, are very particular in what they are allowed to eat. The food is either halal or haram. Haram food is generally all food that is not earned by permissible activities in Islam. Therefore, any food that is stolen or bought using haram money is forbidden. Some earnings e.g. interest and gambling winnings are haram, and so any food bought from such earnings is also haram.

Halal food also means righteous food that has been provided and made edible in the name of Allah. All vegetarian food, dairy produce and seafood are generally permissible, as is game and poultry. But mammals, either land-based or sea-based have to be slaughtered only in the name of Allah (halal) and only certain kinds of animals can be slaughtered.

All carnivorous animals and birds of prey, mammals and birds of reproductive age are haram (cannot be eaten). Beasts of burden that are useful to man, and creatures too small or too young are also forbidden as are all dead animals or birds, but fresh fish (that is dead out of water but not slaughtered) is allowed. Pets should not be slaughtered either. Animals such as pigs, dogs, and members of the cat family are haram.

You cannot mix haram ingredients with halal food either. So, a loaf of bread containing lard combined with a portion of cheese will also become haram. A Muslim can happily eat at a Jewish table but not at one belonging to a Christian, because of these rules.

Slaughtering the animals is a current and emotive issue with the animal welfare lobby. Muslims try to explain that what is haram is the blood of any animal. For blood letting a precise, surgical technique is necessary. Muslims argue that if carried out properly this method is less painful and more humane than other methods such as stunning etc.

Dress

Men, women and children are all are expected to cover their heads for religious acts and ceremonies, although it is only as a mark of respect and is not obligatory. The men wear caps, turbans or anything to cover their heads. Women use a hijab or any other form of head covering to hide their hair. There are no rules as to what clothes or dresses should be worn but there are strict rules for both men and women as to how much of the body must remain covered at all times. Men must cover themselves from their waist to ankles at all times. Women must cover their hair and all their body, from the neck to the ankles. Tight dresses must be avoided. Men are not allowed to wear silk or gold etc., while women can, but only in moderation.

Make up is considered an abuse of natural skin but women are allowed to wear henna patterns on their hands etc. Men can use henna to colour their grey hair. Wearing perfumes is Sunnah, but they should be halal and therefore no alcoholic ingredients are allowed. Tattoos are forbidden.

Muslim men and women must be pure and clean at all times. It is not possible to perform daily prayers five times a day if the body is not clean. There are also rules for bathing and include the stipulation that a Muslim must take at least one shower every day.

Giving of gifts

General

Fruit and flowers are welcome. Cash can be given as a gift to younger people. Gifts ranging from a copy of the Qur'an to a box of chocolates are always welcome but a gift of erotic art, or something that contains images of nudity or any other non-Islamic gift would not be accepted and would cause great offence.

When visiting

It is common for guests to give a gift to their host. This can be anything from flowers to calligraphic writings although it is not a good idea to take food or drink and never take a bottle of wine as any form of alcohol is strictly forbidden. It would be very wrong to talk about pigs or dogs at the dinner table. Presents should always be modest and should never show excessive indulgence.

Gifts for a new born child	Whatever the mother usually needs on this occasion is acceptable.
Wedding gifts	Gifts such as household and electrical goods are welcome as they help young couples start a home and modern practices such as wedding lists are gaining greater credibility. Cash gifts are also acceptable on special occasions such as marriages, births etc. but are always only given by elder relatives to younger ones.
Greetings	Id Mubarak cards are popular and are becoming more easily available in card shops. Muslims in the UK have also begun to follow the custom of giving cards on anniversaries, birthdays, Fathers' Day and Mothers' Day and even Valentine's Day.

Medical treatment

Doctors of the same sex are preferred. Muslim ladies may request a female doctor for certain treatments and would be very offended if a male doctor were to be involved in delivering their babies.

Although there are several exceptions to the established rules of Islam on drugs etc. (for example alcohol is a permitted ingredient in medicines), on matters of transplants or blood transfusions orthodox Muslims may give doctors hard time. However, as the preservation of life is paramount in Islam, these practices should be acceptable. As in Judaism, Islam allows abortions only in certain serious conditions. Euthanasia is totally forbidden in Islam. The use of Muslim corpses in medical schools for teaching purposes is opposed but post mortems to determine the cause of death is acceptable. Generally, in all special circumstances in medicine or otherwise, Islamic laws are very flexible.

Main languages spoken

Arabic is the language of both the Holy Qur'an and all Salah. For all other Islamic activities the language used is the spoken language of the country of residence. Translations of the Qur'an are available in all languages.

Other

There is no caste or class system in Islam. Equality is paramount. An emperor and a slave both stand shoulder to shoulder in prayers and eat from the same plate. There are two main schools of thought in Islam – Sunnis and Shias – but they are all part of one Muslim community. Some extreme forms of Shiaism are not recognised by Sunni Muslims.

There is no priesthood in Islam. Anyone who knows how to recite the Qur'an and knows his Salah (which even a child knows) can lead the prayers. In several families, young sons lead the prayers while the father stands behind his son in the jammat (the straight line of praying people behind the Imam).

Women cannot lead the prayers. There are no monks, nuns or hermits. There may be scholars and pious people, but not saints as such. One can obtain the status of a great Scholar (Imam, Sufi, Wali etc.) by leading a most pious life.

It is recognised that though the prophethood ended with Muhammad (pbuh), the vilyat (sainthood) still continues. This is only an affair between Man and God. Nobody ordains this sainthood. The people themselves realise the piousness and scholarship of such a person and he gets the status by his own piety and intensity of worship. You recognise a saint when you see one.

Homosexual relationships are strictly forbidden in Islam.

Glossary

The Qur'an was revealed in Arabic, therefore Arabic is the language of Islam, Islamic worship, theology, ethics and jurisprudence. Islam is inextricably linked with the Arabic language despite the variety of languages spoken by the believers.

For readers who have not encountered Islamic terms, this transliteration is a simplified version of that used by contemporary scholars. An apostrophe is used to indicate a pause. Note that the words Salah and Zakah end in 'h' when they appear alone. When part of a phrase these words are written with a 't' at the end, e.g. Salat-ul-Zuhr, Zakat-ul-Fitr, as a guide to pronunciation.

Term	Explanation
Adhan	Call to prayer. From the same root, Mu'adhin (one who makes the call to prayer).
Allah	The Islamic name for God in the Arabic language. Used in preference to the word God, this Arabic term is singular, has no plural, nor is it associated with masculine, feminine characteristics.
Angels	Being created by Allah from light. They have no free will and are completely obedient to Allah.
BCE	Before the Common Era. Equivalent to BC in Christianity.
CE	Common Era. Equivalent to AD in Christianity.
Fatwa	The legal guidance of a pious, just, knowledgeable Muslim scholar and jurist, based on the Qur'an, Sunnah and Islamic Shari'ah.
Hajj	Annual pilgrimage to Makkah, which each Muslim must undertake at least once in a lifetime if he or she has the health and wealth. A Muslim male who has completed Hajj is called Hajji and a female Hajjah.

Term	Explanation
Halal	Any action or thing which is permitted or lawful.
Haram	Anything unlawful or not permitted.
Hijab	*Veil (trans.)*. Often used to describe the head scarf or modest dress worn by women, who are required to cover everything except the face and hands in the sight of anyone other than the immediate family.
Id	*Recurring happiness (trans.)*. A religious holiday, a feast for thanking Allah and celebrating a happy occasion. Sometimes spelt Eid.
Id Mubarak	Id blessings! Greeting exchanged during Islamic celebrations.
Id-ul-Adha	Celebration of the sacrifice. Also known as Id-ul-Kabir – *the Greater Id* – and Qurban Bayram (Turkish) *feast of sacrifice*.
Id-ul-Fitr	Celebration of breaking the fast on the day after Ramadan ends, which is also the first day of Shawal, the tenth Islamic month. Also known as Id-ul-Saghir – *the Lesser Id* – and Sheker Bayram (Turkish) – *sugar feast*.

Term	Explanation
Imam	*Leader (trans.)*. A person who leads the communal prayer, or a founder of an Islamic school of jurisprudence.
Iman	Faith.
Islam	Peace attained through willing obedience to Allah's divine guidance.
Jihad	Personal individual struggle against evil in the way of Allah. It can also be collective defence of the Muslim community.
Jinn	Being created by Allah from fire.
Ka'bah	A cube-shaped structure in the centre of the grand mosque in Makkah. The first house of worship for the One True God.
Laylat-ul-Qadr	The Night of Power, when the first revelation of the Qur'an was made to Prophet Muhammad (pbuh).
Makkah	City where the Prophet Muhammad (pbuh) was born, and where the Ka'bah is located. Also known as Mecca.
Mi'raj	The ascent through the heavens of the Prophet Muhammad (pbuh).
Mu'adhin	Caller to prayer. Known in English as 'muezzin'.

Term	Explanation
Muhammad	*Praised*. Name of the final prophet Sometimes spelt as Mohammed or Muhammed (pbuh).
Muslim	One who claims to have accepted Islam by professing the Shahadah.
Qur'an	That which is read or recited. The Divine Book revealed to the Prophet Muhammad (pbuh). Allah's final revelation to humankind.
Ramadan	The ninth month of the Islamic calendar, during which fasting is required from just before dawn until sunset, as ordered by Allah in the Qur'an.
Salah	Prescribed communication with, and worship of, Allah, performed under specific conditions, in the manner taught by the Prophet Muhammad (pbuh), and recited in the Arabic language. The five daily times of Salah are fixed by Allah.
Sawm	Fasting from just before dawn until sunset. Abstinence is required from all food and drink (including water) as well as smoking and conjugal relations.

Term	Explanation
Shahadah	Declaration of faith, which consists of the statement, 'There is no god except Allah, Muhammad (pbuh) is the Messenger of Allah'.
Shari'ah	Islamic law based on the Qur'an and Sunnah.
Sunnah	Model practices, customs and traditions of the Prophet Muhammad (pbuh).
Ummah	Community. Worldwide community of Muslims, the nation of Islam.
Zakah	Purification of wealth by payment of annual welfare due. An obligatory act of worship.
Zakat-ul-Fitr	Welfare payment at the end of Ramadan.

Compiled by S. Ikram Ali

judaism

Judaism

Jew – a person of Hebrew descent or whose religion is Judaism.

An introduction to the faith

Judaism cannot be separated from Jewish life as a whole. According to Jewish belief the 'Torah', containing the laws and commandments by which the Jewish people live, was given directly by one indivisible God to Moses, who in turn handed it down to the Jewish people.

Judaism presents a unique expression of a history, culture and faith united by a desire to lead a constructive and spiritual life in accordance with God's will. It is a way of life maintained by the Jewish people throughout thousands of years, which has in turn kept them alive and fulfilled; living in the present, mindful of the past, but hopeful for the future.

Festivals

Shabbat (Sabbath) is the most important day of the week for Jews, on which Jews are commanded to rest and to keep the day holy. God created the world in six days and rested on the seventh, and the fourth commandment tells us "Remember the Sabbath day to keep it holy." It begins just before sundown on Friday night and ends after dark on Saturday night. Shabbat runs from sundown of the 'previous' day because of the wording of the opening verses of the Torah "And there was evening and there was morning, one day" (Gen.1: 5). Friday night is a customarily 'special' evening with traditional Jewish food and rituals. There are services at many synagogues on Friday nights and Saturday mornings.

Festival dates vary due to the Jewish calendar.

Jewish months are lunar months. Each is 29 or 30 days long and a Jewish year can be between 353 and 385 days long. Accordingly it is necessary to add a full extra 'leap' month seven times in every nineteen civil years in order to align the two calendars.

Whereas the civil calendar year commences in January, the Jewish calendar year begins in September/October and dates from 5761 BCE.

Rosh Hashana

In September or October this is the Jewish New Year and the beginning of a ten-day period of repentance, which ends on 'Yom Kippur'. The Synagogue service starts just before sundown, with a further service the following morning. It is distinguished from all other holy days by the blowing of the 'Shofar', a ram's horn. At the conclusion of the service it is the custom for congregants to wish each other "Shana Tova" – meaning a good year.

One of the customs at Rosh Hashana includes eating an apple dipped in honey to indicate the hope that the coming year will be a sweet one.

Yom Kippur

Usually in October means the Day of Atonement, i.e. the expiation of sin on the part of the sinner and pardon by God. Atonement is made through fasting and prayer. Yom Kippur is a twenty-five hour fast for the purposes of purifying thoughts and of increasing the intensity of repentance. The Yom Kippur fast commences shortly before sundown, and at the end of the following day the fast is over and the service finishes with the sound of the Shofar.

Pesach (Passover)

In March or April. This Festival commemorates the most important event in the history of the Jewish people, namely its rescue from slavery in Egypt. Families and friends gather together to celebrate that deliverance. There are three essential things which distinguish the Passover:
(a) The prohibition of eating, drinking or having in one's possession any food made of 'leavened' (fermented) grain, (b) the obligation to eat 'matza' (unleavened bread) and (c) the celebration of the 'seder' (the ceremony held in the home) at which time the story of Passover is recited.

It is customary for spring cleaning to take place before Passover and the larder must be replenished with new items of food, which are kosher for Passover. Special kosher for Passover dishes and utensils must be used at this time. All the old stock of food is disposed of or given away. All types of flour are prohibited apart from matzo and potato flour, which are used instead. Meat, vegetables and fruit are permissible.

Other significant religious events

T'u B'Shvat	New Year for Trees.
Purim	A Festival when the Book of Esther in scroll form is read in synagogues.
Yom HaShoah	'Holocaust Memorial Day' referring to events that led to the brutal elimination, dispossession, exile or orphaning of several million Jews in the years 1933 – 1945.
Yom Ha'Atzmut	Israel Independence Day.
Shavuot	Commemorating the giving of the Torah and the first Harvest Festival.
Tisha B'Av	The destruction of the Temple and other sad memories.
Sukkot	Temporary dwellings to commemorate the exodus from Egypt. Harvest Festival.
Simchat Torah	The end of Torah readings for the year. The cycle is recommenced with the reading of the first chapter of Genesis.
Chanukah	Commemorating the rededication of the Temple in Jerusalem in 165 BCE.

Birth customs

In traditional belief a child born of a Jewish mother is Jewish by birth. In mixed marriages, if the mother is Jewish and the father is not, the children are still born Jews.

Different customs welcome new babies but the main commandment is circumcision ('Brit Mila' or 'Briss'), on the eighth day after a boy's birth. If a woman's first child is a boy, her husband must redeem the child on the thirty-first day after his birth. The ceremony is called 'Pidyon Ha-Ben' – Redemption of the firstborn son.

Death customs and funeral rites

An appropriate undertaker will take charge of the body and prepare for it burial. Jewish tradition requires funerals to take place as soon as possible but not on the Sabbath. It is not encouraged for mourners to wear totally black clothes or to buy new clothes especially for the occasion. By custom, the mourners put the first spadefuls of earth into the grave and others generally follow suit. It is not customary to send flowers to a funeral. Jewish law stipulates burial as distinct from cremation.

'Shiva' is the seven-day period of mourning. Traditionally, a short prayer service is held at the house of mourning each evening of this period. During a Shiva, family, friends and acquaintances visit the mourners and on leaving, visitors wish each mourner 'long life'. Food, cakes or biscuits with a 'kosher' label are taken to a house of mourning, thus ensuring that there is enough food for mourners in the house. Close friends may provide more substantial meals.

There are many customs and traditions, including the mourners sitting on low stools during the period of Shiva, the covering over of mirrors and the making by mourners of tears or a cut in an item of their clothing to signify their grief. The mourning period is generally for a period of one year after the death during which time a memorial stone is placed on the grave.

Diet

The subject of what foods may be eaten by observant Jews is called 'Kashrut'. The word 'kosher' means fit, acceptable or ritually useable. The opposite is 'tref' or 'trefa', meaning not edible by Jews.

There are three classifications of food, namely meat and meat-containing food ('fleishig'), milk and milk-containing foods ('milchig') and foods containing neither meat nor milk ('parev'). Fleishig and milchig may not be eaten together, but parev may be eaten with either.

The only meat that Jews are allowed to eat is that which comes from animals that both chew the cud and have split hooves. Jews are permitted to eat farmyard fowl, including chickens, turkeys and ducks. The permissible animals must be slaughtered only by a 'Schochet' (a specially qualified person).

Meat must be koshered, i.e. soaked in water and then salted, before consumption, to remove all the blood. The only kinds of fish which Jews are permitted to eat are those which have both fins and scales.

Refreshments

After a Synagogue service refreshments are usually provided, more elaborately so if it is a special occasion. You will not cause offence by declining. However, Jews enjoy food, are enthusiastic hosts and may be quite persistent with their offerings!

Dress code

Head coverings	During synagogue services, all men must keep their heads covered. Most use a headcovering called a 'Kippah' or 'Yarmulka', and married women are expected to wear hats or headscarves. Many orthodox married Jewish women either wear a 'Sheitel' (a wig) or keep their natural hair covered at all times.
Clothes	During a synagogue service congregants should be 'decently' attired. Women should not wear sleeveless dresses, skirts above the knee, trousers or shorts. During a Sabbath service, Jewish men wear a 'Tallit' (prayer shawl), but many Jews also wear 'Tsitsit' (a small garment with fringes) under their shirts every day. Chasidic Jews maintain their traditional black clothing, which is of Eastern European origin. Many observant people do not wear clothing in which wool and linen are mixed – 'shaatnez'.
Shoes	It is traditional not to wear shoes made of leather during Yom Kippur and Tisha B'Av and leather shoes should not be worn by mourners during the first week of mourning.
Tattoos	The Torah forbids tattooing but there are many Jewish survivors who have a number tattooed on their arm by the Nazis.

The giving of gifts

Gifts in general	Fruit and flowers are always acceptable gifts.
Guest gifts	Flowers or a plant is always acceptable, alternatively, a bottle of wine.
Gifts for a newborn child	If in doubt, ask the advice of the new mother.
Wedding gifts	Most couples today have a 'wedding list' or it is quite traditional to give money. If you prefer, ask the hostess for advice.
Greetings	There are Jewish cards available from many outlets and most synagogues have facilities where you can buy such cards and also gifts with a Jewish flavour.

Main languages spoken

The main language for Jews is the spoken language of the country of residence, but Hebrew is the language of prayer in almost all synagogues, being and having been the preferred language for religious writing since Biblical times.

Medical treatment

Preference of the sex of a doctor is usually the choice of each individual but the very Orthodox patient may prefer to be treated by a doctor of the same sex.

Jewish laws on contraception are based on the sanctity of human life and a wife may use contraception if her life may be endangered by pregnancy.

As the preservation of human life is paramount, blood transfusions and necessary donation of organs are considered acceptable.

In Jewish law, therapeutic abortion where the life of a pregnant woman is endangered and also abortion within the first three months of pregnancy, to prevent the birth of a severely deformed child are both permitted.

Euthanasia, or 'mercy killing,' is absolutely prohibited by Jewish law, being considered equivalent to murder.

The use of Jewish corpses in medical schools for teaching purposes is opposed but post mortems, to determine the cause of death, are viewed more leniently.

Names and naming ceremonies

A girl may be given a name in the Synagogue during her first week of life and a boy is given a name at the time of his circumcision.

In addition to its civil name, a child will be given a Hebrew name, followed by 'ben' (son of) or 'bat' (daughter of) his or her father's Hebrew name.

Other

Things that are acceptable	Jewish people find it perfectly reasonable to accept visitors' lack of knowledge about Judaism.
Things that are not acceptable	Forms of anti-Semitism, even in a joking fashion, from someone who is not Jewish.

Jews are divided into three main religious groups, namely Orthodox, Reform and Liberal (Progressive).

Traditional/Orthodox Jews	Accept the revelation of the entire Torah, both written and oral, by God to Moses.
	In a traditional Orthodox synagogue, men and women sit separately, the women usually upstairs or behind a 'Mechitza' – a panel or curtain or even a symbolic division separating men from women.
	Occasionally at ultra-Orthodox functions, men and women may sit together for a meal but the dancing area is divided by a Mechitza, and the men dance with men and the women with women.
Reform/Liberal (Progressive)	The most immediately noticeable differences between Reform and Orthodox congregations are that men and women sit together in Reform congregations and that services are shorter, parts thereof being in English.

Glossary

Most of the terms included in this glossary are Hebrew in origin. However, since the Jewish Diaspora, many terms reflect the different countries where Jews have settled. For example, many words are in Yiddish, a common language (a mixture of German, Russian and Hebrew) developed by the Jews throughout Central and Eastern Europe.

The preferred form of this glossary uses the Sephardic pronunciation, which is equivalent to Modern Hebrew as spoken in Israel today. As with all transliterations, there may be acceptable differences in the ways in which words are spelt.

Preferred Form	Main Variables	Explanation
Aliyah		*To go up (trans)*. (i) being called to read the Sefer Torah in the synagogue. (ii) the migration of the Jews to Israel.
Aron Hakodesh		*Holy Ark (trans)*. The focal point of the synagogue, containing the Torah scrolls
Bar Mitzvah		*Son of Commandment (trans)*. A boy's coming of age at the age of 13, usually marked by a Synagogue ceremony and family celebration.
BCE		Before the Common Era. Equivalent to BC in Christianity.

Preferred Form	Main Variables	Explanation
Bimah		*Dais (trans).* Raised platform primarily for reading the Torah in the Synagogue.
CE		Common Era. Equivalent to AD in Christianity.
Challah	Hallah	Enriched bread used particularly on Shabbat and during festivals.
Chazan	Hazan Cantor	Leader of reading, singing and chanting in the services of some Synagogues.
Cheder		Hebrew lessons, usually held on a Sunday morning.
Gefilte fish		A dish of chopped fish, boiled or fried.
Get		A Jewish divorce.
Hagadah	Haggadah	*Telling (trans).* A book used at Seder (q.v.).
Halakhah	Halacha	*The Way (trans).* The code of conduct encompassing all aspects of Jewish life.
Hanukiah	Chanukiah	Nine-branched Hanukkah lamp used at the Festival of Hanukkah.
Hanukkah	Chanukah	*Dedication (trans).* An eight-day "Festival of Lights" to celebrate the re-dedication of the Temple following the Maccabean victory over the Greeks.

Preferred Form	Main Variables	Explanation
Kashrut		Laws relating to keeping a kosher home and lifestyle.
Kibbutz	Kibbutzim (pl.)	Israeli collective village based on Socialist principles.
Kosher	Kasher	*Fit; proper (trans).* Foods permitted by Jewish dietary laws.
Latkes		Fried potato cakes traditionally eaten on Hanukkah.
L'chaim		*To Life! (trans).* A toast given before taking an alcoholic drink.
Mazeltov		Congratulations! Good Luck!
Menorah		A seven-branched candlestick, which was lit daily in the Temple.
Ner Tamid		*Eternal light (trans).* The perpetual light above the Aron Hakodesh.
Parev	Parveh	Neutral foods, which are neither milk nor meat, e.g. vegetables, eggs, fish.
Pesach	Passover	Festival commemorating the Exodus from Egypt. One of the three Biblical pilgrim festivals. Pesach is celebrated in the Spring.
Pogrom		Organised attack on Jews, especially frequent in 19th and early 20th century Eastern Europe.

Preferred Form	Main Variables	Explanation
Rabbi		*My teacher (trans).* An ordained Jewish teacher. Often the religious leader of a Jewish community.
Rosh Hashanah	Rosh Ha-Shanah	*Head of the Year (trans).* Jewish New Year.
Seder		*Order (trans).* A home-based ceremonial meal during Pesach, at which the Exodus from Egypt is recounted using the Hagadah.
Sefer Torah		Torah scroll. The five books of Moses handwritten on parchment and rolled to form a scroll.
Sephardim	Sefardim	Jews originating from Mediterranean countries, especially Spain, North Africa and the Middle East.
Shabbat	Shabbos Sabbath	Day of spiritual renewal and rest commencing at sunset on Friday, terminating at nightfall on Saturday.
Siddur		*Order (trans).* Daily prayer book.
Synagogue	Shul Bet Haknesset Bet Hamidrash	Building for Jewish public prayer, study and assembly.
Torah		*Law; teaching.* The five books of Moses.

Preferred Form	Main Variables	Explanation
Yiddish		Language used predominately by Jews of Central and Eastern European origin. Some Yiddish words have found their way into common English usage, particularly in the United States.
Zionism		Political movement advocating the return of the Jews to the Land of Israel.

Further reading

Wouk, H., 1959 *'This is My God',* by Herman Wouk, Dell

Hayim Halevy Donin, 1991 *'To Be A Jew'*, Basic Books

Special thanks to:

Rabbi Vivian Silverman and Penny Phillips

Edited by Doris Levinson and Clive Levinson.

sikhism

Sikhism

Faith/Culture

Sikhism is based on the teachings of the first Sikh Guru, Guru Nanak, who was born in the Punjab in India in 1469 CE. His outspoken call and his personal initiatives for equality across class gender, race and faith were revolutionary.

Nine other Gurus followed Guru Nanak as leaders of the faith, the tenth being Guru Gobind Singh. He decreed that after his death the line of human Gurus should end and that instead the Holy Book of the Sikhs, the Guru Granth Sahib, should become the Guru for all Sikhs. Because this scripture has taken the place of the living Guru, it is treated with utmost respect, enjoys the full and highest authority amongst Sikhs and is central to the Sikh way of life, its ceremonies, festivals and code of conduct.

Main languages spoken

Punjabi is the main language for Sikhs although the language of the country of residence is also widely spoken. Altogether in the UK 800,000 Sikhs, Punjabi Hindus and Punjabi Muslims speak Punjabi as their first language.

An introduction to the faith

Sikhs believe:

In one God who created the universe.

In the oneness of humanity, equality of all people, the family of God. This means that God is not interested in what religion people follow but He is concerned with their conduct.

From this follows the belief that God is not exclusive to any one religion, but that different religions are following different paths to the same Reality. Sikhs believe that any one person has the right to follow their chosen path and that everyone should respect other faiths.

Equality of women. Since the time of Guru Nanak Sikh women have enjoyed complete equality with men.

Service to the wider community (Sewa). Sikhs are expected to participate in community service and to share some of their earnings with others, not just other Sikhs.

In leading his or her life in three dimensions, all of which have equal importance. These are: nam japna (to worship only the almighty), kirat karna (earning one's livelihood by one's own efforts) and vand chakna (sharing one's time, talents and earnings with the less fortunate).

Festivals

The main festivals celebrated by Sikhs are:

The birthdays of Guru Nanak and Guru Gobind Singh.

The martyrdom of Guru Arjan and Guru Tegh Bahadur.

Baisakhi.

Diwali.

These significant religious events in the Sikh calendar are observed in the gurdwara (Sikh temple) when prayers are offered and kirtan (hymns) are recited. The story of the event is narrated and in some cities where there is a large Sikh population there may be street processions. Sikhs do not believe that any one day is any more holy than any other but on the actual date of the anniversary in the UK a special service will be held in the gurdwara with the main celebration being held the weekend following.

All the above events are preceded by an akhand path, a continuous reading of the Guru Granth Sahib, which takes around 48 hours and which is timed to reach its conclusion on the morning of the festival day. The martyrdom anniversaries are not treated as days of grief but of inspiration.

Baisakhi

Is celebrated in April and commemorates the birth of the Khalsa. It is at this festival that new Sikhs are initiated. It also signifies the harvest festival in the Punjab and marks the first day of the Sikh year. Processions and feasting follow the reading of the Guru Granth Sahib.

Diwali

The festival of light, which is also celebrated by Hindus, is important to Sikhs because it commemorates the freedom from Mughal captivity of the sixth Guru, Guru Har Gobind. Gurdwaras and homes are illuminated with coloured lights and small oil lamps called 'divas' and gifts are exchanged between family members and friends.

The Birth of Khalsa (The Sikh Identity)

The word 'Khalsa' means the community of the pure and its membership is made up of Sikhs who have undergone the sacred Amrit Panth ceremony. Guru Gobind Singh initiated this on Baisaiki Day in 1699 when he instituted the first five Sikhs into the Khalsa Panth, the community of initiated Sikhs.

The ceremony involves the drinking of amrit (a sanctified liquid of sugar crystals and water) in the presence of five Khalsa Sikhs as well as the Guru Granth Sahib.

The physical symbols that denote a Khalsa Sikh are known as the 5 Ks of Sikhism, each of which is of spiritual and practical significance. They are known as the 5 Ks because the Punjabi for each word (kakka) begins with the 'k' sound. They are:

The Kesh

Long, uncut hair that is a symbol of spirituality. The Kesh reminds a Khalsa to behave like the Gurus and shows acceptance of God's will.

The Khanga

A comb which is a symbol of cleanliness and orderliness.

The Kara	A steel bracelet worn on the right wrist as a reminder of the need for restraint in deed and in remembrance of God at all times.
The Kirpan	The double-edged ceremonial sword as a symbol of dignity and the Sikh struggle against injustice. It is worn purely as a religious symbol and not as a weapon.
The Kachera	Knee-length undershorts worn as a symbol of self-control and chastity.

Keshdhari is the name given to Sikhs who do not cut any of their body hair and wear a turban whether or not they have taken Amrit. Those who believe in Sikhism but have not yet been initiated or who have let their practice lapse are sometimes known as Sahajdhari (literally, 'slow adopters').

Birth customs

Although there is no religious ceremony when a baby is born, the child is taken to the gurdwara by its parents for prayers and a blessing. Usually Amrit is prepared and a few drops of this holy water are poured into the mouth of the child, the remainder being taken by the mother. This ceremony can also take place in the family home.

At the time of the visit to the gurdwara a prayer of thanksgiving is offered and hymns of thanksgiving are sung. Sometimes akhand path is held. A personal name for the child is also chosen *(see Names and naming ceremonies)*.

Death customs and funeral rites

At the deathbed of a Sikh, the relatives and friends console themselves and the departing soul by reading from the Guru Granth Sahib especially Sukhmani, the Psalm of Peace. When death occurs no loud lamentations are allowed. Instead Sikhs chant Waheguru, Waheguru (Wonderful Lord). On death close family relatives wash the body of the deceased. Sikhs are cremated (with the five Ks, if possible). Men are cremated wearing the turban. Following a laying-in period at the family home the coffin is closed and then taken briefly to the gurdwara before going on to the crematorium.

In the UK, where there are modern crematoria with electric or gas furnaces, it is usual practice for the deceased to be taken to the crematorium for cremation. After the prayers, the eldest son and some close relatives of the deceased are allowed to have the last touch, according to tradition, by pushing the coffin into the furnace, witnessed by close family members.

The bereaved family, for the comfort of their own souls as well as for the peace of the departed, start a reading of the Guru Granth Sahib, which may be at their own house or at a neighbouring gurdwara. Friends and relations also take part. After a week or so they again come together when the reading is finished. The usual prayer is offered and karah parshad (holy sweet pudding made from flour, butter and sugar) is distributed.

The remains of deceased Sikhs in the UK are often taken to Kiratpur in Punjab (India) and scattered into the Sirsa Nadi river. However, some Sikhs do scatter the remains in an area of river especially designated for this purpose.

It is forbidden to erect monuments over the remains of the dead, although suitable monuments in their honour at any other place would be quite permissible.

Diet

Dietary restrictions are a matter of conscience and religious belief for each individual Sikh. However, no Sikh is permitted to eat halal meat (meat that has been killed in the Muslim way) and consumption of beef is forbidden, since the cow is a sacred animal. The majority of Sikhs are vegetarian.

Sikhs who are initiated as members of the Khalsa are not allowed to partake in the use of alcohol, tobacco, drugs, or other intoxicants and should not eat any meat, fish or eggs. However they are permitted to eat dairy products.

When a ceremony is held in the gurdwara the food, which is always vegetarian, is prepared in the communal kitchen, the langar, and served to anyone who wishes to eat.

Dress

Both Sikh men and women dress modestly and to some Sikhs any exposure can cause offence.

Sikh men mainly wear Western dress but are advised to keep the turban and kachera. A long, loose shirt known as a kurta is mainly worn at home along with loose trousers known as pyjamas, and a turban.

Sikh women always cover their whole bodies. Traditional dress is the shalwar (a trouser-like garment for the legs) and a kameez (tunic) with a chunni or dupatta (headscarf). The shalwar and kameez is often worn as day and nightwear. The wearing of a traditional Western nightdress when in hospital could cause embarrassment when being visited by relatives and so the patient should be allowed to continue wearing traditional dress.

The wearing of the Kirpan (sword) by Sikh women and men signifies that they are initiated Sikhs, and this should not be removed. Sikh women in hospital would be very keen to continue wearing their Kirpan and so every effort should be made to allow them to do so.

When visiting the gurdwara a non-Sikh should ensure his or her head is covered. Shoes must be removed and placed in the racks provided. It is also advisable to cover the legs.

At religious events, the congregation traditionally wears orange, dark blue or yellow clothing.

The traditional dress for a Sikh bride is a red bridal gown with gold or silver jewellery, whilst the groom wears Western dress and a turban, and is veiled in flowers.

White is the colour of mourning.

Giving of gifts

Gifts in general	Fruit and flowers are always acceptable as is a gift of money.
Gift for a newborn baby	Generally gift vouchers, clothes or money.
Wedding gifts	It is traditional to give money (or ask the family for advice).
Greetings	Normal cards for the occasion (i.e. birthday cards, wedding day cards etc as available in all card shops).
	A Sikh should greet other Sikhs with the salutation "Waheguru Ji Ka Khalsa, Waheguru Ji Ke Fateh (Hail Khalsa of the Wonderful Lord who is always victorious) or Sat Sri Akal (God is Truth).
Accepting an invitation	It is permissible for Sikhs to accept an invitation even if it involves him or her going to a place of worship different from that which he or she normally attends as long as a belief in the Sikh faith is maintained.

In the gurdwara

It is a tradition that men and women sit separately in the main hall (diwan or darbar) and in the dining hall (langar), but it is not essential. At weddings men and women sit together. After services in the gurdwara everybody is offered karah parshad. It is very rude not to accept it.

Medical treatment

Treatment by a male or female doctor is a personal choice but some Sikh ladies may prefer a lady doctor for certain treatments.

Sikhism promotes family planning through self-control. Abortion is against Sikh ethics.

Sikhs consider the saving of human life to be a priority so blood transfusions and necessary donations of organs are usually considered acceptable.

Names and naming ceremonies

Traditionally the name of a new baby is chosen at the gurdwara by opening the Guru Granth Sahib at random and reciting the first paragraph on the opened page. The first letter of the first word is given to the family and then a name beginning with that letter is chosen and announced to the whole congregation.

The tradition of using family names was dropped at the time of Guru Gobind Singh because it identified the caste structure, which Sikhs do not recognise. However, in the UK many Sikhs add on their family name to fall in line with the British system that allows the identification and retrieval of records via the family surname.

As well as their personal and family names all Sikh men have the religious name of Singh, which means lion, whilst Sikh women have the religious name of Kaur, which means princess. An example of a Sikh family using a family name as well as a personal name and religious name would be as follows, with the family name following Singh or Kaur i.e.

Husband	Satvinder Singh Toor
Wife	Beljeet Kaur Toor
Son	Indirjeet Singh Toor
Daughter	Kuldeep Kaur Toor

However, Sikhs do not have to take their father's or husband's name but are individuals in their own right. An example of a family using its traditional naming system would be:

Husband	Satvinder Singh
Wife	Beljeet Kaur
Son	Indirjeet Singh
Daughter	Kuldeep Kaur

When traditional names are used it is important that records are kept to maintain identification by using the system in the Punjab i.e. when referring to the wife the registration would be: Mrs Beljeet Kaur (wife of) Mr Satvinder Singh.

Glossary

Sikh terms are drawn from the Punjabi language, and the versions below are based upon that language. Many of these terms will also be found in books on Hinduism and Buddhism but with somewhat different meanings. As with all translations, there are problems that are difficult to resolve.

This is particularly true when moving from the Gurmukhi script, which has an alphabet of 35 letters, to the Roman alphabet, which has only 26 letters. Names of persons and places are only included in this list if variant forms are commonly used.

Preferred Form	Main Variants	Explanation
Akhand Path		Continuous reading of the Guru Granth Sahib from beginning to end.
Amrit		Nectar (trans.) sanctified liquid made of sugar and water, used in initiation ceremonies.
Amrit ceremony	Amrit Sanskar, Amrit Pahul, Khande di Pahul. Sometimes just 'Amrit' or 'Taking Amrit' ('Amrit Chhakna')	The Sikh rite of initiation into the Khalsa. 'Baptism' should not be used.

Preferred Form	Main Variants	Explanation
Anand karaj	Anand Sanskar	*Ceremony of bliss (trans.)* Wedding ceremony.
Ardas		*Prayer (trans.)* The formal prayer offered at most religious acts.
Baisakhi	Vaisakhi	A major Sikh festival celebrating the formation of the Khalsa, 1699 CE.
BCE		Before the Common Era. Equivalent to BC in Christianity.
CE		Common Era. Equivalent to AD in Christianity
Chanani	Chandni	Canopy over the scriptures, used as a mark of respect.
Chauri	Chaur	Symbol of the authority of the Guru Granth Sahib. Fan waved over the scriptures, made of yak hairs or nylon. It should not be called a 'fly whisk'.
Granthi		Reader of the Guru Granth Sahib, who officiates at ceremonies.
Gurbani	Bani, Vani	Divine word revealed by the Gurus. The Shabads contained in the Guru Granth Sahib.
Gurdwara	Gurudwara	Sikh place of worship. Literally the 'doorway to the Guru'.

Preferred Form	Main Variants	Explanation
Gurpurb	Gurpurab	A Guru's anniversary (birth or death). Also used for other anniversaries, e.g. the installation of the Adi Granth, 1604 CE.
Guru		Teacher. In Sikhism, the title of Guru is reserved for the ten human Gurus and the Guru Granth Sahib.
Guru Arjan		The fifth Guru, who was the first Sikh martyr (1563 – 1606).
Guru Gobind Singh	Guru Govind Singh (Original name: Guru Gobind Rai).	Tenth Sikh Guru. It is important to note that the title 'Guru' must be used with all the Gurus' names. Sikhs usually use further terms of respect, e.g., Guru Gobind Singh Ji or Guru Nanak Dev Ji.
Guru Granth Sahib	Adi Granth (Granth' by itself should be avoided).	Primal collection of Sikh scriptures, compiled by Guru Arjan and given its final form by Guru Gobind Singh.
Guru Har Gobind	Guru Hargobind, Guru Hargovind	Sixth Sikh Guru.
Guru Har Krishan Guru Harkishan	Guru Harkrishan	Eighth Sikh Guru.
Guru Nanak		The first Guru and the founder of the Sikh faith (1469 – 1539).

Preferred Form	Main Variants	Explanation
Guru Tegh Bahadur		The ninth Sikh Guru who was martyred for the principle of religious tolerance (1622 – 1675).
Karah parshad	Karah Prasad	Sanctified food distributed at Sikh ceremonies.
Khalsa		*The community of the pure*. The Sikh community.
Khanda		Double-edged sword used in the initiation ceremony. Also used as the emblem on the Sikh flag.
Mela		*Fair (trans)*. Used of Sikh festivals that are not gurpurbs.
Mool Mantar	Mul Mantar	*Basic teaching; essential teaching (trans)*. The basic statement of belief at the beginning of the Guru Granth Sahib.
Nishan Sahib		Sikh flag flown at gurdwaras.
Panj kakke		*The five K's*. The symbols of Sikhism worn by Sikhs.
Panj piare	Panj Pyare (other forms may also be found)	*The five beloved ones*. Those first initiated into the Kalsa; those who perform the rite today.
Panth		The Sikh community

Preferred Form	Main Variants	Explanation
Punjab	Panjab	*Land of five rivers (trans)*. The area of India in which Sikhism originated.
Sandhsangat	Sangat	Congregation or assembly of Sikhs.
Sewa		Service to humanity.
Shabad	Sabad, Shabd	*Word (trans.)* Hymn from the Guru Granth Sahib; the divine word.
Sikh		*Learner; disciple (trans.)* A person who believes in the ten Gurus and the Guru Granth Sahib, and who has no other religion.
Waheguru		*Wonderful Lord (trans.)* A Sikh name for God.

Further reading

C. Shackle, 1981 *A Guru Nanak Glossary*, Heritage Publishers, New Delhi.

Fauja Singh Kirpal Singh, 1976 *Atlas: Travels of Guru Nanak*, Punjabi University, Patiala.

Gopal Sing (Tr.), 1989 *Siri Guru Granth Sahib*, World Book Centre, New Delhi

Harbans Singh (Editor in Chief), 1992 *the Encyclopaedia of Sikhism*, Punjabi University Patiala, Vol.1

H S Singha, 1989 *Mini Encyclopaedia of Sikhism*, Hemkunt Press Delhi,

J P Singh Oberoi, 1975 *The Five Symbols of Sikhism* in perspective of Guru Nanak, (Ed) Harbans Singh Punjabi University, Patiala

Kahan Singh Nabha, *Mahan Kosh, (Encyclopaedia of Sikh Literature)*, Bhasa Vibhag, Punjab.

Khushwant Singh, 1991 *A History of Sikhs*, Oxford India, Paperbacks 2 Vols.

Compiled by Shaminder Singh Bedi and Narinderjit Singh Thandi

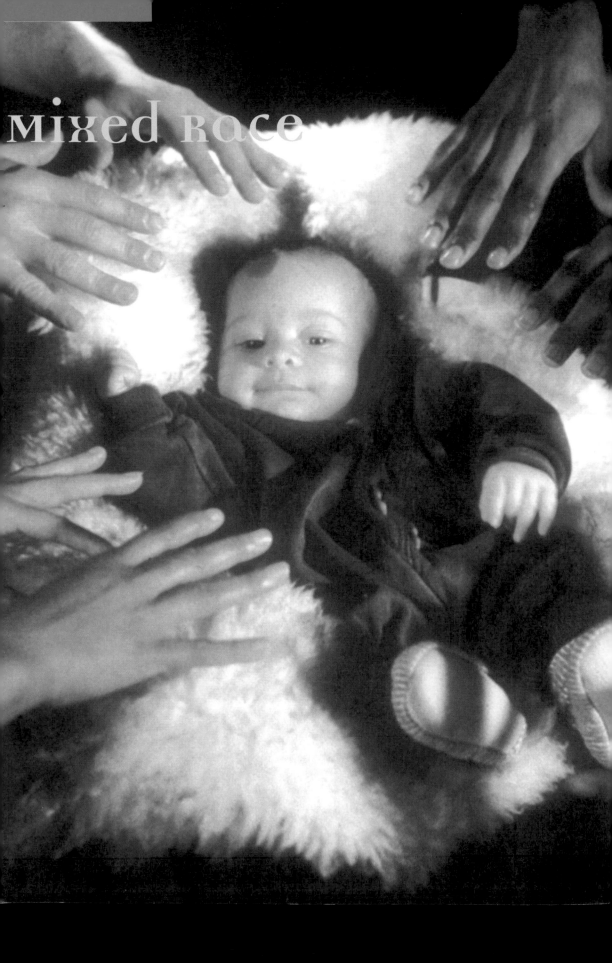

mixed race

Mixed Race

Diversity and the construction of 'Race'

The inclusion of a section on 'mixed race' in a Cultural Diversity Guide illustrates the reality of contemporary British society in both positive and negative ways. In positive terms, it highlights the diversity of the British population and the fact that relationships are formed across racialised boundaries. In negative terms, it indicates that divisions still exist between groups classified as discrete 'races' on the basis of physical characteristics.

The diversity of the population in Britain can be traced back many centuries to the Angles, Celts, Danes, Huguenots, Jutes, Picts, Romans, Saxons and Vikings. Today's heterogeneity encompasses nationality, 'race', ethnicity and religion. The British have Irish, English, Welsh and Scottish nationalities as well as racial/ethnic origins that are African, Caribbean, Arab, Bangladeshi, Bengali, Chinese, Guyanese, Indian, Latvian, Lithuanian, Pakistani, Polish, etc. Their religious affiliations include Bahá'í, Buddhism, Christianity, Judaism, Islam, Rastafarianism and Sikhism, among others.

Notwithstanding this diversity, notions of racial differences did not come into common currency in Britain until people with brown skins settled here. This happened when the Second World War caused Britain to turn to its colonies and former colonies for help, first to fight the war and subsequently to rebuild its devastated economic and material infrastructure. People from the Caribbean and the Indian sub-continent responded, adding a non-European dimension to the existing mixture of races, cultures and religions that comprised British society. In the process, the category of 'mixed race' was constructed to describe the children of unions which crossed the racialised divide between black and white people.

Race versus ethnicity; colour versus culture

Physical and cultural differences between human beings have existed for thousands of years, yet the concept of 'race' has only been in use for about 500 years (Fryer, 1984). 'Race' is a social (or political) construct, which is meaningless in scientific terms, given that more than 94% of the differences that exist between people do so between people of the *same*, rather than different 'races'. To know someone's racial origin only confirms the obvious: that there are physiological differences between people – a fact that tells us nothing meaningful about individuals.

Ethnicity, on the other hand, refers to social attributes, to the cultures that are associated with particular groups: beliefs, customs, language, values, etc. – their ways of life. Culture refers to everything that is not innate: we are not born with a culture, but learn it from our parents, local community and wider society. And though culture includes reference to history and tradition, in today's global world we are all exposed to, and influenced by, many different cultures – through television, books, newspapers and the fact that we live in heterogeneous societies made up of a variety of cultures.

All this means that culture is dynamic; it changes over time and through interaction with other cultures. Thus, notions of a 'pure' culture are as meaningless as those of a pure 'race' – a fact which the black sociologist, Paul Gilroy, explains well:

"...no single culture is hermetically sealed off from others. There can be no neat and tidy pluralistic separation of racial groups in this country. ...Culture, even the culture which defines the groups we know as races, is never fixed, finished or final. It is fluid, it is actively and continually made and re-made" (Gilroy, 1990).

Racial and cultural diversity: myth or reality?

What has been said so far has far reaching implications. Since a person's racial heritage tells us nothing about him or her as a person the sooner the concept is removed from our vocabulary the better. Terms such as 'mixed race' are not only deeply offensive to the people so categorised, but are potentially dangerous because they encourage racialised thinking. And in a world in which the holocaust, apartheid and ethnic cleansing are within living memory, the consequences of this need no reiteration.

The notion of cultural diversity is more complex because, despite change over time, cultural differences between groups do exist sometimes – though by no means always – linked to ethnicity. Some differences stem from people's class or geographical location, ethnic origin or religious affiliation.

"There are differences in life-style, values and attitudes between someone who lives in a castle and someone who lives on an inner city council estate; between the residents of a remote village in the Hebrides and those of central London; between people whose ancestors are African, rather than Polish, Indian rather than English, or Irish rather than Scottish; between people whose religion is Muslim rather than Catholic, or Hindu rather than Jewish." (Macey, 1998)

The above differences are real (though not immutable). However, other presumed cultural differences are myths that rely for their continued existence on selective memory, distorted history and racial stereotyping. This applies particularly to distinctions, which are made between groups defined as black or white (or Asian), where racism results in the exaggeration of difference and the denial of similarity. This can push people who experience racism to turn 'inward', rather than outward and to emphasise a black and/or ethnic identity. In this sense it can be argued that black, Asian and mixed race cultures unite and give strength to people who see themselves as suffering similar forms of oppression.

This is not to suggest that anyone has a singular, racial or cultural identity – no one is only black or white: we are all gendered and class located, as well as individual. Nor is it to suggest that a black, or mixed, identity is no more than a defensive strategy. On the contrary, the assertion of a black culture and/or black identity can be highly positive, as Hyder notes: "Inevitably 'black' will form a significant part of any mixed race person's identity, not just in reaction to white racism but also as a celebration of cultural heritage".

However, he goes on to say: "But it is equally important for mixed race people to express the positive side of their 'white' heritage and just as importantly to celebrate the dynamic nature of their dual heritage" (1993).

Celebrating diversity: The concept of 'dual heritage'

The term 'dual heritage' is used to acknowledge the combination of factors which produce individuals whose parents are from different racial or ethnic or cultural backgrounds. It is a term of celebration – of diversity, individuality and sheer humanity. It is a proclamation of the fact that there is no such thing as a 'pure' race: there is simply one human race of which we are all members. For even if at some point in time in certain parts of the world, people were from closely related gene pools, this stage of human history is long gone for the vast majority of the human family.

"We are all of mixed race and we are all of mixed cultures; isn't it time that we started saying long and loud that this is the norm, this is humanity – and we're proud of being who and what we are?" (Macey, 1998)

Glossary

Black	Used to describe people from African and African/Caribbean backgrounds and is also a political term for people who are not white.
Ethnicity	Relates to culture and focuses on learned characteristics such as beliefs, language and sense of peoplehood (or shared identity).
Interracial	Used to describe a mix of 'races' or relationships between 'races'.
Race	Used to describe groups of people with specific and clearly identifiable characteristics.
Racism	The belief that discrimination against a person on the basis of race or ethnic grouping is justified.

The following terms are some that are, or have been, used to describe people or families whose origins are described as being from different 'races'. None of the terms can be considered 'right' but people's personal preferences should be listened to. It should not be assumed that one person's preference is right for all.

Biracial

Black mixed parentage

Black mixed race

Dual heritage	
Half-caste	still in use but is considered a derogatory term by many.
Mixed heritage	
Mixed parentage	
Mixed race	
Mulatto	still in use but considered a derogatory term by many.
Multiracial	

References

Fryer P. (1984) Staying Power: *The History of Black People in Britain*, London: Pluto Press

Gilroy P. (1990) 'The End of Antiracism 'in Ball W. & Solomos J. [eds] *Race and Local Politics*, London: Macmillan

Hyder R.M. (1993) 'Mixed-Race People in British Society: A Study of Ethnicity and Identity', M. Sc. *Dissertation*, Bradford, University of Bradford

Further reading

Alibhai-Brown Y. & Montague A. (1991) *The Colour of Love*, London: Virago Press

Macey M. (1998) *Transracial Adoption: What's the Problem?*, Berks: People in Harmony

Tizard B. & Phoenix A. (1992) *Black, White or Mixed Race?: Race and Racism in the Lives of Young People of Mixed Parentage*, London: Routledge

Compiled by Marie Macey, People in Harmony

People In Harmony is an interracial anti-racist organisation which promotes the positive experience of interracial life in Britain today and challenges the racism, prejudice and ignorance in society. The organisation believes that the cultural diversity of our society enriches us all, everyone has a right to define their racial and cultural identity and that racism should always be challenged.

General further reading

Further reading

As well as the additional resources listed at the end of each chapter there are a number of useful publications providing further information and references. These include:

Festivals in World Religions, Woodward, P. (ed), Religion and Moral Education Press, Norwich

Shap Calendar of Religious Festivals, Gould, C., Rose, D., Woodward, P. (eds), Shap Working Party, London

The Shap Calendar of Religious Festivals is available from the Shap Working Party, c/o The National Society's RE Centre, 36 Causton Street, London SW1P 4AU. Tel: 020 7932 1190.

The views and opinions expressed in this book are solely those of the authors and do not necessarily represent those of Granada plc.

Acknowledgements

This book would not have been possible without the support and assistance of a great many people who gave their time so freely and willingly, especially the authors of each chapter and those members of the various faith communities who have advised throughout.

Special thanks are due to David Rose, who played the role of mentor and advisor. David taught Religious Education for sixteen years in London schools, followed by two years as advisory teacher for RE in ILEA. He is the author of many books on RE for schools and has written various articles for educational journals. He is currently Director of Teaching Studies in the Faculty of Education at the University of Surrey Roehampton.

Grateful thanks are also due to the Qualifications and Curriculum Authority (QCA) for permitting the use of 'Religious Education – A Glossary of Terms' in the production of this guide. This glossary was produced to give guidance to key words and their meanings and to try to reach some form of consensus on spellings. Included in the chapter glossaries are words that do not appear in the main body of the text. These additional words are included to give the reader a wider knowledge of key words that may prove useful if further study is followed.

Finally thanks to Katie and Layla who inspired this guide and to whom it is dedicated.

Elaine Johnson, Editor